Six new AMERICAN HERITAGE JUNIOR LIBRARY books are published each year. Titles currently available are:

Thomas Jefferson and his World

Discoverers of the New World

Railroads in the Days of Steam

Indians of the Plains

The Story of Yankee Whaling

To Charles
April, 1964
Bob and JoAnn

THOMAS JEFFERSON

AND HIS WORLD

ILLUSTRATED WITH PAINTINGS, PRINTS, DRAWINGS
AND PHOTOGRAPHS OF THE PERIOD

The wax seals with which Jefferson fastened all his letters carried his initials as well as the inscription: "Rebellion to tyrants is obedience to God."

THOMAS JEFFERSON AND HIS WORLD

by the editors of AMERICAN HERITAGE
The Magazine of History

narrative by HENRY MOSCOW
in consultation with DUMAS MALONE
author of *Jefferson and His Time*

Published by

AMERICAN HERITAGE PUBLISHING CO., INC., NEW YORK

Book Trade Distribution by

GOLDEN PRESS · NEW YORK

FOREWORD

THOMAS JEFFERSON appears to have been half a dozen men rolled into one. Most of his mature life was devoted to public affairs, and he held public offices ranging from county magistrate in Virginia to President of the United States. But—besides being a legislator, a diplomat, an executive—he was a farmer, a scientist, an architect, an inventor, a patron of education and the arts. He loved books and believed in people. Most of all he believed in freedom. He was no soldier, like George Washington, but he fought for what he believed in. He was no orator, like Patrick Henry or Daniel Webster, but he was a remarkably good writer. His words have become famous and are quoted around the world.

In his own day, far more people liked him than disliked him, and many idolized him, but some people hated him. Hardly anybody hates him now, except dictators, and he can no longer be thought of as the private possession of any political party. The shrine to him in the city of Washington shows that he belongs to all the American people, just as Abraham Lincoln does. He is now fully recognized as one of the most important figures in our history, and as one of the greatest champions of human liberty in the history of any country. His memory and his wonderful words are cherished by all who value the freedom and dignity of individual human beings throughout the world.

This book tells about the most important things that Jefferson did in his long and active life, but, most of all, it tells about him as a person, recapturing the man and his time in words and pictures. Since he was such a many-sided person, something in him will appeal to practically everybody, regardless of age or locality. This book is a colorful introduction to him and his world, and by means of it readers can begin to get acquainted with one of the most interesting men who ever lived. To the outward view, his world was very unlike our own; but men are still struggling for the freedom he championed, and in spirit he is still very much alive.

DUMAS MALONE

LIBRARY OF CONGRESS CATALOG CARD NUMBER: 60-11827

Designed by Artists and Writers Press, Inc. Printed in the U. S. A. by Western Printing and Lithographing Company. Published by American Heritage Publishing Co., Inc., 551 Fifth Avenue, New York 17, N. Y.

Virginia tobacco is being barreled for shipment to England in this 18th century print. Tobacco planting, begun by John Rolfe in 1612, was colonial Virginia's chief source of wealth, and is the state's leading industry today.

CONTENTS

THE PLANTER'S SON
(1743-1762)

Under the full spring moon, the Cherokees listened in solemn silence by their fires. Their great chief Ontasseté was saying farewell. Tomorrow he would start across the sea to talk with his father, the Great King, in England. The copper skins and black hair of the Indians contrasted with the freckled face and reddish hair of a lean, six-foot senior student from nearby William and Mary College, who stood nearby.

Most white men were there that night in Williamsburg, Virginia, in 1762, out of curiosity. But to the student, Thomas Jefferson, the chief was an old friend. Ontasseté often stayed at the Jefferson's house when tribal business took him from his people's lands deep in the mountains of the interior—to Williamsburg, colonial Virginia's capital.

For as long as Jefferson could remember, he had been interested in the Indians. As a boy of ten, Tom had explored an abandoned Indian village and collected arrowheads.

Everybody knows that Thomas Jefferson wrote the Declaration of Independence. But Thomas Jefferson was also, among other things, an inventor, architect, musician, scientific farmer, diplomat, lawyer, surveyor, astronomer, mathematician, anthropologist, and botanist.

He had a knowledge of Latin, Greek, Italian, French, and Spanish. He founded a great university, the University of Virginia, and a great political party, today's Democratic Party. Jefferson was also President of the United States for an eight-year period, in which the country's size doubled.

The public schools we go to, the denominations of the coins we use, the liberties we take for granted, these things and many, many more we owe in one way or another to the astonishing man who was born on

Foxhunting was a favorite sport of colonial Virginia's Tidewater planters. Hunters, horses, and hounds are seen gathering at dawn for the start of the chase.

April 13, 1743, in a simple four-room house at Shadwell, Virginia.

Jefferson's father was a bright, brave man of great strength. His mother was a gentlewoman born of one of the most distinguished families in the province. Virginia was a lovely and happy land.

For as much as 100 miles in from the Atlantic, Virginia lies flat. When the tide runs shoreward, the sea surges up the great rivers—the Potomac, the Rappahannock, the York, and the James—pushing their current into reverse twice a day. The water brims onto the land and thus gives it the name Tidewater.

On the Tidewater's west, gentle hills swell from the plain: this is the Piedmont. Beyond the Piedmont, parallel ridges of mountains, the Appalachians, range from northeast to southwest. The Blue Ridge is the easternmost ridge of the Appalachians; it looks down, to the west, on the Shenandoah Valley.

The Tidewater produced gentlemen planters; the Piedmont, pioneers. Thomas Jefferson was heir to both heritages.

George III had ruled two years when Ontasseté (left) visited London in 1762.

The Tidewater of Jefferson's youth had been made rich by slaves and tobacco. The great plantations existed because of profitable trade and easily available workers. The frontiersmen of the Piedmont supported themselves and their families by working small farms. The first permanent settlers, who came from England with Captain John Smith in 1607, had quarreled, suffered, and struggled after they established Jamestown in a malarial marsh, and it was not until 1612 that Pocahontas' husband, John Rolfe, tempted by Indian example, set out some tobacco. Two years later Rolfe experimentally shipped some to England. Tobacco had first been introduced to England by Sir Walter Raleigh. Soon England was buying all the tobacco Virginia could produce. A Dutch ship unloaded twenty Negro slaves at Jamestown in 1619, and the next year Virginia had 40,000 pounds of tobacco to ship. By 1628, it had 500,000 pounds.

For almost a century and a half, tobacco was better than money in Virginia. When Thomas Jefferson was born, Church of England ministers still drew their salaries in tobacco, and brought suit when the people tried to make them take money instead.

In 1745, when Jefferson was two years old, the amount of tobacco Virginia had for sale had risen to 38,000,000 pounds. But the sea captains from England who sailed up the rivers and docked their ships at the plantations' wharves were glad to get every pound of it. It paid, of course, for the cargoes the planters had ordered: silks and silver, pots and pianos, axes and hoes, and spices and books and wines.

In the Piedmont, where Jefferson was born, and in the mountains be-

Joshua Fry and Jefferson's father, Peter, surveyed the mountain wilderness of

yond the Piedmont, things were different. A man rode a horse through dark forest, instead of a coach and six on a decent road. If the tangle grew too dense, he had to dismount and hack his way to his destination.

Tobacco, indirectly, was the reason men moved out of the comfortable Tidewater to the forested hills. Tobacco quickly exhausted the fertility of the land. And after John Smith's first settlers, others had come first by the score and then by the hundred. Some, too poor to pay the six pounds sterling passage money, agreed to work without wages a few years for wealthier colonists who advanced the fare. They often planned to move on to the Piedmont to start their own farms when they had worked off their debts.

By royal grant—which other colonies and France disputed—Virginia extended from the Atlantic to the Mississippi, from the Ohio River to the Great Lakes. Virginia also held without dispute the areas which are now Kentucky and West Virginia.

Thomas Randolph's plantation, Tuckahoe (above), stands not far from Richmond. Inside its little schoolhouse (below) where Thomas Jefferson studied, his autograph remains on the plaster wall.

western Virginia in 1749 and mapped the Virginia-North Carolina borderline.

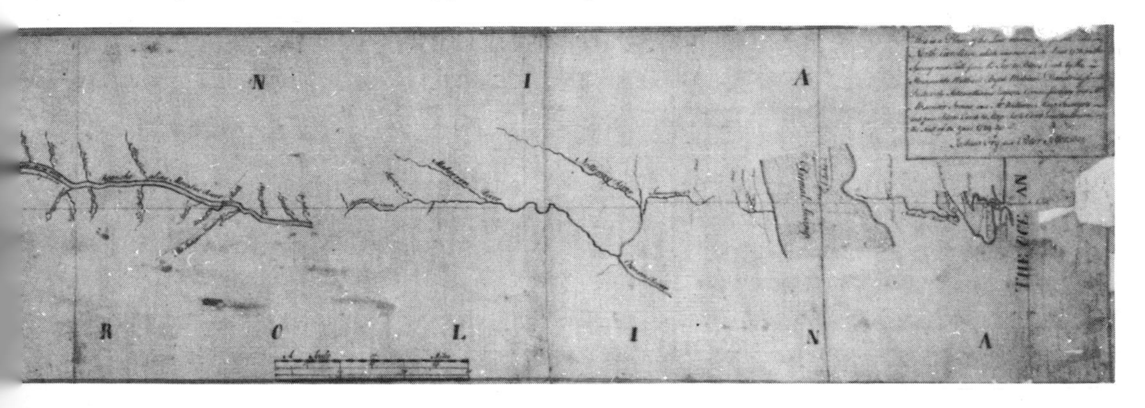

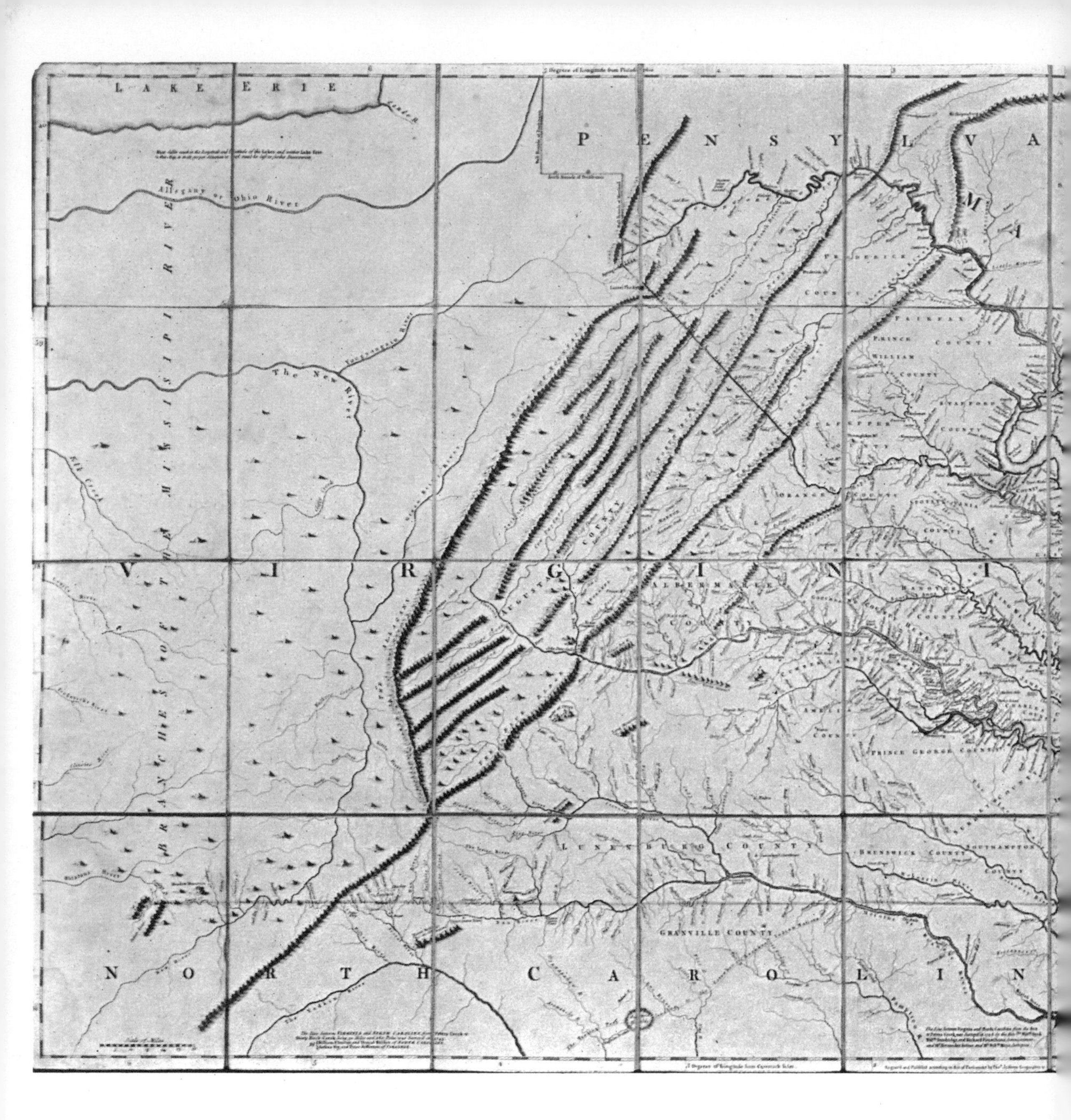

Soon after Jefferson's birth, the British and the French began fighting their third war in half a century over North America's territory. Between wars, nothing slowed the land rush. For land, one applied to Virginia's royal governor, who ruled the colony with an appointed council and an elected House of Burgesses.

If the land did not belong to the Indians and if the governor and his advisors were satisfied that the applicant was a solid citizen with a reasonable request, he generally got a "patent" on the land he wanted.

Such lands had to be surveyed. Surveying was an exciting and profitable business. It attracted men like Thomas Jefferson's father, Peter,

Peter Jefferson and Joshua Fry knew the Blue Ridge mountains so well that the governor of Virginia asked them to draw this map, in 1751. It was the first to show the mountains in parallel ranges.

who was a surveyor, a tobacco planter, and an eager and successful applicant for land patents.

Peter Jefferson was so strong he could stand between hogsheads of tobacco lying on their sides and raise them upright, two at a time. Each weighed 1,000 pounds.

Peter had no schooling because there was none available and his mother, who might have taught him, had died when he was eight. He taught himself many things, however, and was chosen with Joshua Fry, a professor of mathematics at William and Mary College, to survey the boundary line between Virginia and North Carolina. He also worked with Fry on one of the first maps of Virginia. Peter Jefferson also knew that there was more to surveying than mathematics. Accompanied by Thomas Lewis, Jefferson also made a surveying trip into western Virginia to mark the boundaries of Lord Fairfax's land.

But Thomas Jefferson's father was not a simple frontiersman. His family had prospered since the first Jeffersons arrived in America from Wales in 1612. The first House of Burgesses, convened in 1619, included a Jefferson. Peter's father had left him a fair-sized tract in Goochland County, along with a few horses, slaves, and some livestock.

Peter Jefferson married his best friend William Randolph's cousin, Jane Randolph, in October 1739. She was the daughter of Isham Randolph, Adjutant General of Virginia, a wealthy, well-educated, widely traveled man. The Randolphs had first come to Virginia in 1674 and were related to many of the most famous families in the colony, including that of George Washington.

Several years before Peter married, he and his friend William Randolph each acquired several thousand acres of wilderness on the Rivanna, a stream that flows into the James. Long afterward, Thomas Jefferson wrote proudly of his father: "He was the third or fourth settler, about the year 1737, of the part of the country in which I live."

When Peter wanted to build a house for Jane, he found that the best spot lay on William's side of the stream. So William genially signed over two hundred acres to Peter, exacting in return only the largest bowl of arrack punch that was served in Williamburg's Raleigh Tavern. Later, he threw in another two hundred acres, this time for fifty pounds sterling. Thus Peter got a site to build Shadwell, the house where Thomas Jefferson was born.

Thomas Jefferson's earliest memory was of leaving Shadwell, when he was about two. A slave on horseback bore him on a pillow for seventy miles along wilderness trails to William Randolph's pleasant Tidewater estate, Tuckahoe. Randolph, dying, had begged of Peter Jefferson one final act of friendship: to move to Tuckahoe, run the plantation, and raise and educate Randolph's son, Thomas Mann, and Thomas Mann's sisters, Judith and Mary, who were already motherless.

Shadwell was more difficult to get to and from than Tuckahoe was. Ocean-going ships could not sail up the Rivanna River. Tobacco had to be shipped by wagon, or rolled along the trails in strongly built hogsheads to a wharf.

At Tuckahoe Thomas Jefferson got his first schooling, with the three Randolphs and Tom's four sisters, Jane, Mary, Elizabeth, and Martha.

Life at Tuckahoe was fun. The house, unlike Shadwell, was large and splendid. Approaching it, one passed through an avenue of great elms. Gardens surrounded it. It was built on a hill and had a beautiful view of the James.

Frequently there were guests to greet and to admire when they came to dance in Tuckahoe's salon, with its huge chandelier, and there were dancing lessons for the young people themselves.

When the Jeffersons finally moved back to Shadwell, Tom was sent off to the Latin school, run by a crusty Church of England clergyman, Mr. William Douglas.

Home in Shadwell for vacations, Tom rode in the forest, swam and fished in the Rivanna, and roamed the hillsides with his beloved sister Jane, who was three years older. He delighted in his father's volumes of Shakespeare, Swift, and Addison.

He first hunted alone when he was ten; to make him self-reliant, his father sent him out into the forest with a gun. Tom got nothing

When tobacco was shipped from Shadwell by way of the shallow Rivanna River to the James, it moved in two canoes lashed together, called "double canoes."

and was fairly well discouraged until he discovered a wild turkey in a pen. Using a garter, he tied the bird to a tree, shot it, and proudly took it home.

When he was fourteen, his father rescued him from Mr. Douglas and sent him to the log house school of the Reverend James Maury, a clergyman of Huguenot ancestry who had great enthusiasm for Latin and Greek. Tom soon became friends with a classmate, Dabney Carr.

Quite suddenly, Tom had to become a man. The summer that Tom was fourteen, his father died, not quite fifty years old.

In the next year and a half, Tom proved himself wise beyond his years. By January, 1760, he had decided to go to college rather than continue private study. He had the support of one guardian, Peter Randolph, in this plan. He convinced his other guardian, John Harvie, to agree to the plan by sending him a letter on January 14, 1760, in which he explained his reasons for wanting to go to William and Mary.

"In the first place, as long as I stay at the Mountain, the loss of one-fourth of my Time is inevitable, by Company's coming here and detaining me from School. . . And on the other Hand by going to the College, I shall get a more universal Acquaintance, which may hereafter be serviceable to me: and I suppose I can pursue my Studies in the Greek and Latin as well there as here, and likewise learn something of the Mathematics. . ." Harvie agreed and in the spring of 1760, Thomas Jefferson set out, stopping on the way at the home of Colonel Nathaniel West Dandridge of Hanover County. It was at one of Colonel Dandridge's parties that he met a neighbor of Dandridge who at twenty-four had already gone bankrupt as a storekeeper, but who fiddled and danced and jested with an enthusiasm that entranced young Jefferson. The fellow had studied law only six weeks but was confident he could pass the examinations for admittance to the bar and he delighted Jefferson with a promise to look him up in Wil liamsburg. As Jefferson finally rode off to William and Mary College he could not know that the life of the gay young fiddler, Patrick Henry, would be closely linked with his own in the historic days to come.

This picture of an unnamed early Tidewater plantation shows a great house,

slave cabins, barns, warehouses, a water mill, and a tobacco ship ready to sail.

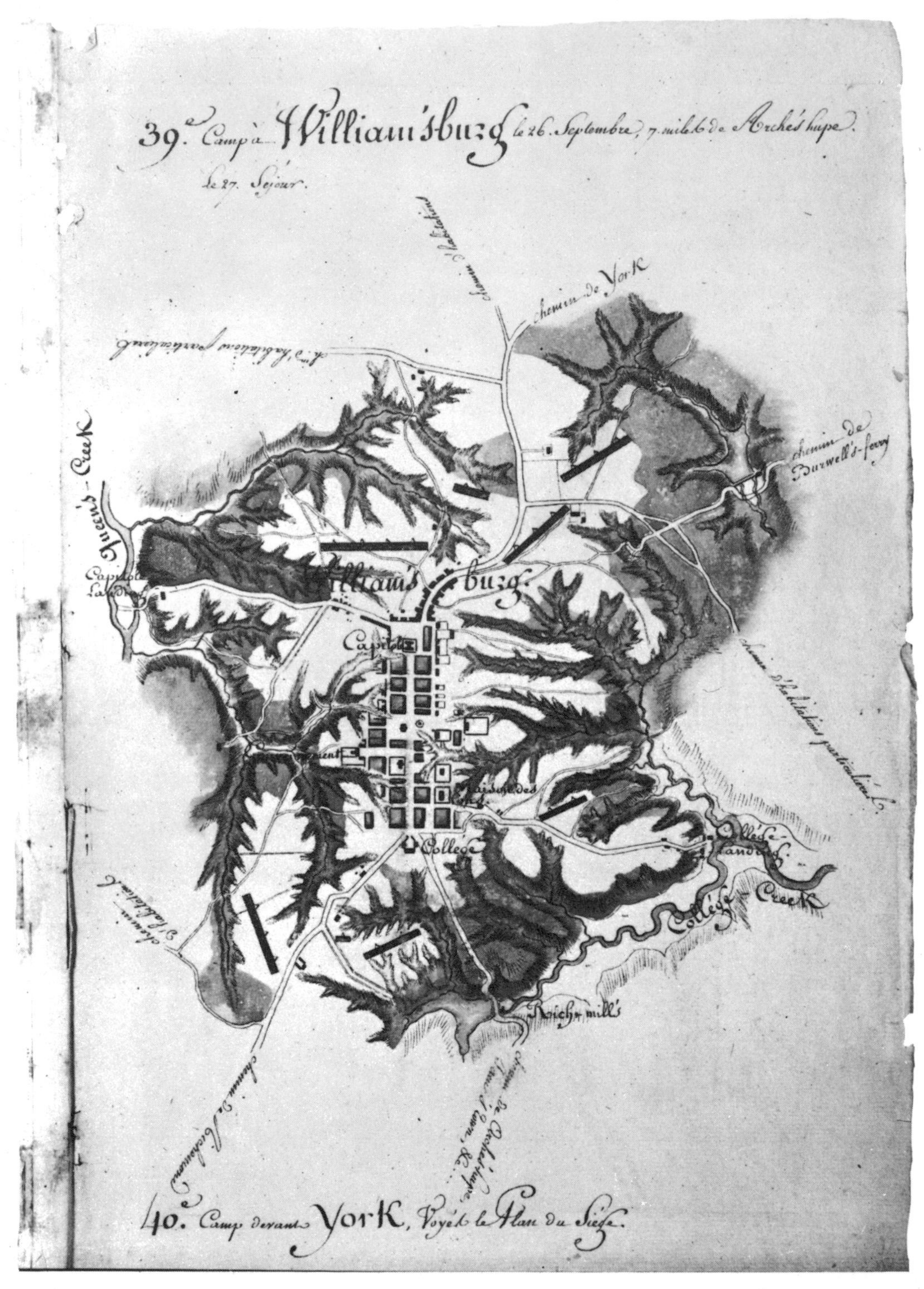

This map of Williamsburg was made in 1780, twenty years after Jefferson enrolled in William and Mary College. Duke of Gloucester Street runs from the college to the Capitol; the Governor's Palace is at left center. The town—named for King William III—was first settled in 1633, and became the second capital of colonial Virginia in 1699, the year the first capital, Jamestown, burned.

A STUDENT IN WILLIAMSBURG
(1760-1769)

The royal arms of colonial Virginia.

Riding into Williamsburg a few days before his seventeenth birthday, Jefferson found the college disappointing and the town a delight. Williamsburg was the biggest community he ever had seen.

A visiting graduate of Oxford, describing it at the time, was less impressed, writing: "It consists of about two hundred houses, does not contain more than one thousand souls and is far from being a place of any consequence."

Tiny it was, but it turned out to be a place of much consequence, and it was rarely dull. Planters spending the winter in town often found actors from London on hand to amuse them with Shakespeare and the lively comedies of Congreve and Wycherley. There were dice to roll, cards to deal, good wines to drink, and excellent dinners to eat in the elegant and expensive Raleigh Tavern. There were horse races, cockfights, wrestling matches, fiddling contests, singing contests, even beauty contests.

Handsome six-horse coaches churned the sand-and-oyster-shell surface of the 100-foot-wide, three-quarter-mile long main street, on which the college stood at one end and the capitol at the other.

William and Mary College was made up of a grammar school, an Indian school where a few young redskins placidly resisted the white man's wisdom, a philosophy school, and a divinity school. All told, the college had fewer than one hundred students. The main building, sixty-six years old when Jefferson arrived, was built on the great Sir Christopher Wren's design.

The housekeeper was carefree and the faculty had to warn her to stop serving scraps for supper. Few students took seriously the ban on keeping race horses or fighting cocks; their dogs, their guns, sometimes their slaves shared their rooms.

There were supposed to be six professors at the college, all but one of whom were Church of England clergymen. But two of them, in a most high-spirited mood, rallied their students for a brawl with the town boys and lost their posts. Two or three others were suing the college's trustees and were in England demanding justice when Jefferson arrived in Williamsburg.

Fortunately the college had one professor who was worth a whole university to Jefferson. He was a Scot named William Small, only nine years older than Jefferson, and the only non-clerical member of the faculty. He had, Jefferson says, "an enlarged and liberal mind." He had the unconventional idea that a teacher should not beat a student. Small began teaching Jefferson and his classmates mathematics, but as the faculty dwindled, he took on everything from grammar to physics and astronomy.

That first year in college, Jefferson rarely missed a horse race or a play, where the audience sometimes included the handsome 28-year-old colonel named George Washington who was serving his first term as a burgess. Jefferson danced as graceful a minuet as anybody at the Raleigh and at its end could kiss a lady's hand with no sign of seventeen-year-old bashfulness.

But he differed from other young men in Williamsburg. His thirst was for knowledge, not wine. His questions in class and his conversation out of class so impressed Dr. Small that he made Jefferson his close friend. He introduced him to other close friends, George Wythe (pronounced "with") and Francis Fauquier, the royal governor.

Wythe, a courtly man, had overcome poverty to make himself, by the time he was thirty, the best Latin and Greek scholar and one of the busiest and most respected lawyers in Virginia. He was, however, thought to be a bit eccentric: at the first opportunity, he freed his slaves and provided for their futures.

Governor Fauquier was as gay as he was learned and wise. A Londoner, he was a member of the Royal Society; he had accomplished the astonishing feat of writing an interesting, successful book on taxation; he was kindly, generous, liberal in his views, and, "with some allowances" as an early historian put it, "he was everything that could have been wished for by Virginia under a royal government."

Fauquier loved company and soon Jefferson was dining elegantly at the palace once a week with the governor, Small, and Wythe, and playing his violin or a cello in Fauquier's chamber music concerts. At the dinners, Jefferson said that he had

Before William and Mary (below) was opened in 1694, as an Episcopal school and Indian mission, Harvard was the only college in the thirteen colonies.

In Williamsburg's Bruton Parish Church (above) hangs Virginia's Liberty Bell, which rang out to proclaim Virginia's independence from Britain in May, 1776.

heard "more good sense, more rational and philosophical conversation, than in all my life beside."

Jefferson always felt that knowing Dr. Small "probably fixed the destinies of my life" and he took Small and Wythe and one other man, his kinsman Peyton Randolph, for his models. "In a moment of temptation or difficulty I would ask myself, 'What would Dr. Small, Mr. Wythe, Peyton Randolph do in this situation?' " He omitted Fauquier because the governor loved to gamble and Jefferson disapproved of gambling, even forbidding his slaves to own dice or cards.

Despite the important friends he had made, Jefferson was far from satisfied with himself at the end of his first college year. He wrote to his guardian that he had spent too much on fun and finery, and that the costs should be deducted only from his share of the inheritance, not from the whole estate. His guardian, who knew many young men of worse behavior, told Jefferson not to worry.

But, home in Shadwell for vacation, Jefferson began studying in earnest, tumbling out of bed as soon as dawn dimly lit the clock on the mantel. He kept at his books all day and often read until 2 A.M.

It is probably to the Wythe house, on Williamsburg's Prince George Street, that William Small brought young Jefferson to meet the distinguished George Wythe.

Sometimes, taking a book along, he would cross the Rivanna in his canoe and climb to a hilltop where he planned to build a house. (After he had learned Italian, he named the hill *Monticello*, which, in Italian, means "Little Mountain.") If Dabney Carr—who himself was about to enter William and Mary—was visiting Shadwell, the two of them would read and talk, and sometimes roast a partridge for dinner, under a great oak on the hill. They came to love the tree so much that they agreed that when one of them died, the survivor would not fail to bury his dead companion beneath the tree.

Back in college for his senior year, Jefferson maintained the same pace. Almost abandoning company, horseback riding, and even the violin, he studied fifteen hours out of twenty-four. Some advice he wrote out for two friends provides a good look at Jefferson's idea of a well-spent day. "Till Eight o'clock in the morning," he recommended, one should study agriculture, chemistry, anatomy, zoology, botany, ethics and religion.

"From Eight to Twelve read Law. . . From Twelve to One, read Politics. . . . In the Afternoon read History." (He specified Ancient, Modern, English, and American.) And "From Dark to Bedtime" he suggested should be devoted to poetry, drama, and literary criticism, with Shakespeare's plays and Demosthenes' and Cicero's speeches as required reading.

At twilight, Jefferson gave himself a little relaxation. He would run to a stone a mile beyond the town limits, then run back.

Jefferson had his goals in life fixed firmly in his mind. When he was graduated from William and Mary in the spring of 1762—soon after he heard Chief Ontasseté's memorable speech—he was able to read Greek and Latin well and was able to get along in French and Italian, and was anxious to learn German and Spanish. He had read the ancient philosophers in their own tongues, and probably had already begun to read such moderns as John Locke and Montesquieu.

He knew a lot about the sciences. He had collected a library of hundreds of distinguished books in a land where few men owned more than a Bible. At nineteen, he was one of the best educated men in Virginia. For this, he could credit Peter Jefferson, Maury, Small, Wythe, and Fauquier. He could also credit his own philosophy: "It is wonderful how much may be done if we are always doing."

The next thing to be doing was to become a lawyer; planting was profitable, but hardly provided mental exercise. Dabney Carr was going to be a lawyer, too. So was their friend John Tyler (whose son John became President of the United States). Patrick Henry, though he had failed at farming and innkeeping as well as shopkeeping, already was one: to the horror of one examiner, George Wythe, and the astonishment of others, he had passed the Virginia bar examination after six weeks' study.

There were no law schools. To become a lawyer, one went to work for a lawyer and read his law books, ran some of his errands, helped prepare his briefs, watched him in court. So Dr. Small arranged for Wythe to teach the law to Jefferson.

Jefferson's lifelong friend, John Page.

It was the perfect choice, and though Wythe later taught John Marshall, and had Henry Clay for a secretary, Jefferson remained his favorite pupil and his lifelong friend; when Wythe died, he left Jefferson his library.

Patrick Henry's informal approach to the law—successful enough for him—was not for Jefferson, though the two were good friends and Henry lived with Jefferson whenever he was in Williamsburg. Jefferson's study of the law lasted all of five years. For he was determined to know not only what the law said, but whether the Romans, the French, or the ancient Saxons had written it in the first place. He had to see how it had been phrased in the original, which meant in the case of Saxon laws that he had to master the Saxon language, which was then obscure and forgotten. He considered whether laws still made sense, or ought to be amended or repealed. Whenever he came across an interesting law, an important legal decision, or an impressive philosophical idea, he copied it into what he called a *Commonplace Book*. Jefferson's book eventually had hundreds of detailed entries.

Sharing rooms in Williamsburg, Jefferson and John Tyler studied far into the night. When their roommate, Frank Willis, stabled his horse in the cellar and came upstairs after a gay evening, he sometimes had to upset their table and spill their lawbooks to make them stop studying. But Jefferson was finding time also to manage the plantations, practice at the violin three hours a day, ride his horse daily, make and record meteorological and astronomical observations (a habit he had acquired from Fauquier), dine out, go to balls, attend the theatre, and, of course, be on hand when interesting cases were being tried in court.

Jefferson was on hand for a case that was not only interesting but significant. It involved his old teacher Maury, the university professors who had been suing William and Mary when he entered college, and Patrick Henry.

George Wythe (above) was a close friend of brilliant Francis Fauquier (right) who was royal governor of Virginia (1758–68).

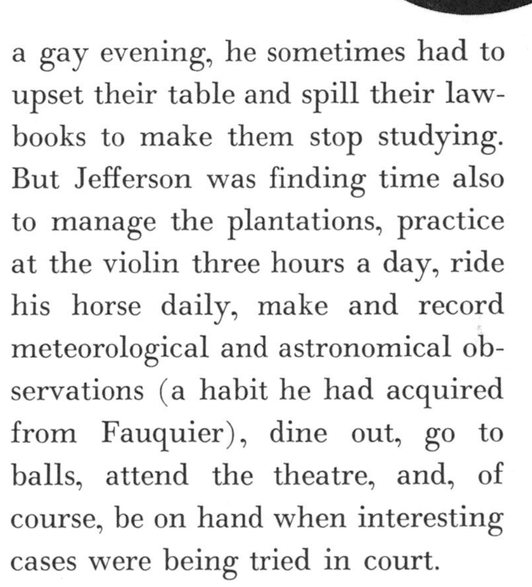

George Wythe and Thomas Jefferson must often have walked through this gate at the garden entrance to the Governor's Palace, on their way to visit Fauquier.

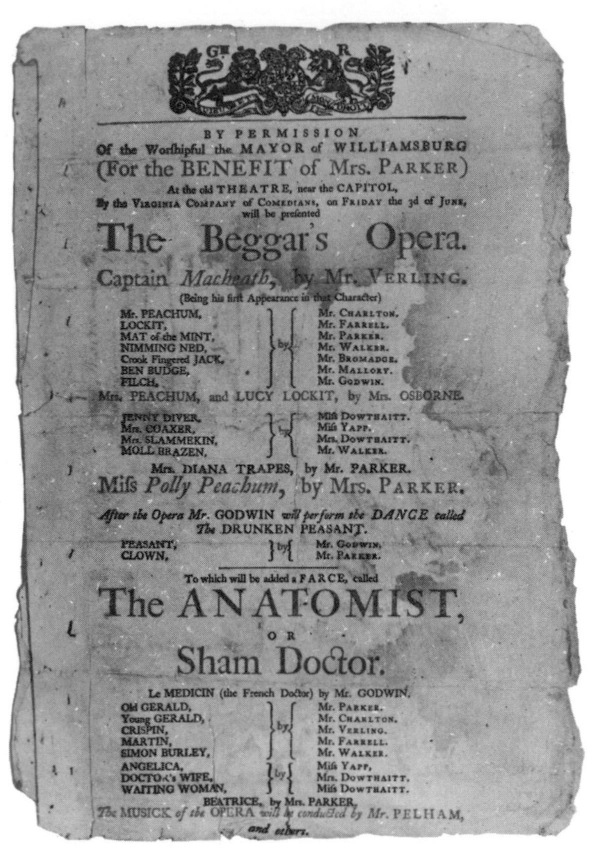
G R

BY PERMISSION
Of the Worshipful the MAYOR of WILLIAMSBURG
(For the BENEFIT of Mrs. PARKER)
At the old THEATRE, near the CAPITOL,
By the VIRGINIA COMPANY of COMEDIANS, on FRIDAY the 3d of JUNE,
will be presented

The Beggar's Opera.

Captain *Macheath*, by Mr. VERLING.
(Being his first Appearance in that Character)

Mr. PEACHUM,	by	Mr. CHARLTON.
LOCKIT,		Mr. FARRELL.
MAT of the MINT,		Mr. PARKER.
NIMMING NED,		Mr. WALKER.
Crook Fingered JACK,		Mr. BROMADGE.
BEN BUDGE,		Mr. MALLORY.
FILCH,		Mr. GODWIN.

Mrs. PEACHUM, and LUCY LOCKIT, by Mrs. OSBORNE.

JENNY DIVER,	by	Miss DOWTHAITT.
Mrs. COAXER,		Miss YAPP.
Mrs. SLAMMEKIN,		Mrs. DOWTHAITT.
MOLL BRAZEN,		Mr. WALKER.

Mrs. DIANA TRAPES, by Mr. PARKER.
Miss *Polly Peachum*, by Mrs. PARKER.

After the Opera Mr. GODWIN *will perform the DANCE called*
The DRUNKEN PEASANT.

PEASANT,	by	Mr. GODWIN.
CLOWN,		Mr. PARKER.

To which will be added a FARCE, called

The ANATOMIST,
OR
Sham Doctor.

Le MEDICIN (the French Doctor) by Mr. GODWIN.

Old GERALD,	by	Mr. PARKER.
Young GERALD,		Mr. CHARLTON.
CRISPIN,		Mr. VERLING.
MARTIN,		Mr. FARRELL.
SIMON BURLEY,		Mr. WALKER.
ANGELICA,	by	Miss YAPP.
DOCTOR's WIFE,		Mrs. DOWTHAITT.
WAITING WOMAN,		Miss DOWTHAITT.

BEATRICE, by Mrs. PARKER.
The MUSICK *of the* OPERA *will be conducted by Mr.* PELHAM,
and others.

Jefferson was in Williamsburg when these plays were acted. He probably saw them, as he liked to go to the theatre.

The argument dated back to 1758, when Jefferson was studying with Maury, who was an Anglican clergyman. The Church of England was the only recognized church in Virginia as it was in the Mother Country, and though perhaps half the population belonged to other denominations, everyone was taxed to pay the Anglican ministers' salaries, according to the English practice.

These salaries were payable in tobacco. But the 1758 tobacco crop was scant. Prices were up and the value of money down. So the hard-pressed Burgesses voted to pay the ministers in cash, a twopence per pound of tobacco due them. The clergy protested. Fauquier upheld the Burgesses. The William and Mary professors sailed to England to complain.

In London, the King's Privy Council decided in favor of the ministers and finally, in 1763, old Maury sued to recover in cash the market value of 16,000 pounds of tobacco. The jury had only to say how much he should get. The decision would affect all other ministers, too.

The Burgesses hired Patrick Henry as their lawyer. Henry was not an elegant speaker. He said *larnin'* for learning, and *nateral* for natural. "Whenever the courts were closed for the winter season," Jefferson wrote afterward, "he would make up a party of poor hunters of his neighborhood, go off with them to the piny woods of Fluvanna, and pass weeks in hunting deer, of which he was passionately fond, sleeping under a tent, before a fire, wearing the same shirt the whole time, and covering all the dirt of his dress with a hunting shirt."

As a lawyer, he was too lazy to prepare his cases, and he demanded his fees in advance on the ground that he kept no books. But, as Jefferson said, "his powers over a jury were so irresistible that he received great fees for his services."

This was his first great case and Jefferson was there to listen; undoubtedly they had discussed the issues many a night in Jefferson's rooms. The court was jammed. Henry started badly but soon warmed up and denounced the ministers so passionately that they left the courtroom. Then he denounced the King. His Majesty had forfeited all right to the people's obedience, Henry contended, by letting his Privy Council veto their legislature's act. When the ministers' attorney protested that "the Gentleman has spoken treason," Henry only grew more daring.

The jury was out five minutes. It awarded Maury one penny. In wild excitement, the crowd bore Henry off on its shoulders, probably to Jefferson's rooms.

The clergy of Virginia actually had established law on their side, but the verdict was intended as a warning to the British government and to the King, George III, who took a more active part in that government than the previous two Georges—George I and George II—had taken.

Virginians were loyal subjects of George III and considered themselves Englishmen. But when a Virginian said "My country" he meant Virginia, and Virginians had been making most of their own decisions for a long time.

Jefferson was to play an important part in Virginia's struggle to keep the right to make her own decisions.

Jefferson danced quadrilles, like this one, at parties in Williamsburg.

THE PENMAN OF THE REVOLUTION
(1770-1776)

King George III

Young Mr. Jefferson the lawyer, as he entered the General Court in Williamsburg, knew he would be opposing his old friend George Wythe, one of the colonies' best attorneys. He knew that, win or lose, his client could not pay and that his chances of winning were small.

Jefferson's client was a mulatto named Samuel Howell. Howell's great-grandmother had broken a law passed in 1705. The churchwardens, to punish her and admonish others, had condemned her infant daughter to thirty-one years of slavery. The girl grew up and, while she was still a slave, bore a daughter, who was Samuel Howell's mother. Howell's mother, too, was a slave, because another law, passed in 1723, extended the penalty to her. Now, in April, 1770, Samuel Howell was a slave, still paying for his ancestor's offense. He had asked Jefferson's help, and Jefferson was suing to compel Mr. Netherland, Howell's owner, to free him.

John Murray, Lord Dunmore

"I suppose," Jefferson said in court, "It will not be pretended that the mother being a servant, the child would be a servant also under the law of nature" because "under the law of nature all men are born free" and "everyone comes into the world with a right to . . . . the . . . . personal liberty . . . . given him by the author of nature."

Jefferson argued that the law of 1705, which had enslaved Howell's grandmother, had been intended to punish wrongdoers, "not to oppress their innocent offspring." The 1723 act which enslaved Howell's mother was wrong. Neither act justified enslaving Samuel.

"Wythe, for the defendant, was about to answer," Jefferson recorded later, "but the Court interrupted him and gave judgment in favor of his client." Samuel Howell remained a slave.

But Jefferson did not lose many cases, and, riding from county court to county court, he was a busy lawyer. His clients ranged from poor men like Howell to William Byrd, one of the richest of Virginians.

Until a few weeks before *Howell v. Netherland* was tried, Jefferson lived at Shadwell with his mother, his invalid sister Elizabeth, and the twins Anna Scott and Randolph, who were twelve years younger than he. Mary had been married for ten years. Martha had married Dabney Carr. Jefferson's sister, Jane, had died.

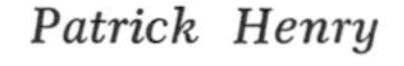

Patrick Henry

Peyton Randolph

By 1770, Jefferson's quiet plantation life was completely upset. He had been appointed justice of the peace and elected burgess. He had traveled and he was building Monticello: a house the like of which Virginia had never seen.

And Jefferson had still another interest. The Rivanna was not navigable by cargo craft, and Peter Jefferson had not been able to ship tobacco from Shadwell. When he reached twenty-one, Jefferson deftly ran his canoe on a survey voyage through waters swirling around the rocks that obstructed the stream. The rocks, he decided, could be cleared. He got the legislature to approve the project and he was working with the country's leaders, raising funds, and letting and supervising contracts. Soon the river was free of rocks.

Years later, shortly before he was elected President, Jefferson asked himself whether his life had bene-

Samuel Howell's trial took place here, at Hanover County Courthouse, in 1770.

fited his country, and to find the answer he wrote down his accomplishments. The clearing of the Rivanna River was listed along with the writing of the Declaration of Independence.

After he got the Rivanna project underway, he set out, at twenty-three, on a visit to New York. The first day his horse ran away twice, nearly killing him. The second day he was drenched by a two-hour downpour, for houses were miles apart on wilderness roads. The third day, when he was fording a stream, the water rose to the cushion of his

Williamsburg's Raleigh Tavern.

one-horse carriage and one wheel mounted a boulder. When he finally reached Philadelphia, he spent his time with many of the city's leading thinkers and—although it was then thought to be a very dangerous procedure—he had himself inoculated against smallpox.

While traveling through the colonies on his way to New York, Jefferson encountered British shillings, Portuguese crowns, Spanish dollars or "pieces of eight," Dutch ducatoons, French écus, and Louis d'or which were in use as regular American currency. To complicate things, each colony printed its own paper currency. The confusion of cash was a nuisance and Jefferson wished he could eliminate it. Twenty years later, he did.

Jefferson was always busy with more than one project or interest at a time. The building of Monticello began in 1767, the same year that Wythe, introducing him to the General Court, transformed him from student to lawyer. Jefferson had 68 cases that year—a huge number for a fledgling—and in the fall session alone he had to appear at Staunton, Orange Court House, Culpeper Court House, Winchester, Fauquier Court House, and Richmond. But at Monticello he managed to find time to supervise the construction of his house.

After Governor Fauquier died, George III appointed the Right Honorable Norborne Berkeley, Baron de Botetourt, to be governor of Virginia.

Following a truly regal reception when he arrived in Williamsburg from London in October, 1768, Botetourt properly called for elections for the House of Burgesses. Jefferson decided to run for a seat in the House. Although he was only twenty-five, he was already a man of standing. His project of clearing the Rivanna River had impressed people. Despite the fact that he limited his campaigning to providing punch for all who wanted it at Shadwell —which was near Charlottesville courthouse where the voting took place—he won the election easily.

The house at Shadwell burned on February 1, 1770. The fire was a good reason for speeding the work up on Monticello, and by November, a little brick cottage, a tiny part of the plan, stood ready for Jefferson. About the time Jefferson moved into the cottage, he met Martha Wayles, a young widow and the daughter of a fellow lawyer, John Wayles of The Forest plantation.

Soon Jefferson was sending his servant Jupiter to the Williamsburg theater to hold seats for two. He often visited her home, The Forest, to play the fiddle while Martha played the harpsichord.

His new interest in music made Jefferson dissatisfied with his old violin. He knew of a splendid violin, but it belonged to cousin John Randolph and John would not sell it. But Jefferson made such a pest of himself that the cousins finally drew

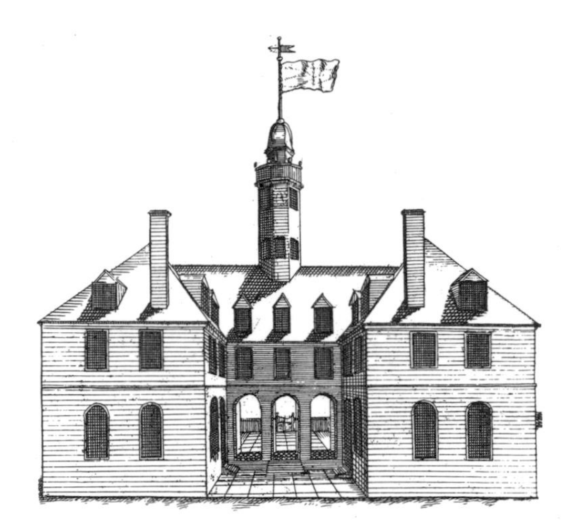

Patrick Henry denounced the Stamp Act here in Virginia's House of Burgesses.

up an imposing document, witnessed by Patrick Henry and George Wythe, and celebrated the signing at the Raleigh. If Randolph died first, Jefferson got the violin. If Jefferson died first, Randolph could choose two hundred pounds worth of his friend's books. Jefferson acquired the violin long before his cousin died, and it was a sad day for both when he did.

There was no sadness, only gaiety, at The Forest on New Year's Day, 1772, when Thomas Jefferson and Martha Wayles Skelton were married. The newlyweds stayed on at The Forest for a fortnight, then set out for Monticello.

On the morning after he returned to Monticello with his bride, Jefferson wrote in his *Garden Book*, where he kept a careful record of the growth of his gardens and orchards at Monticello and of the weather:

Jan. 26. the deepest snow we have ever seen. In Albemarle it was about 3.f. deep.

Jefferson's wedding to Martha Wayles Skelton, at The Forest in 1772, probably

Jefferson and Martha began their marriage in troubled times. The troubles stemmed from the Seven Years War, as it was called in Europe, or the French and Indian War as it was called in America. By the 1763 Treaty of Paris which settled the peace, King George acquired both India and Canada from France, and Florida from Spain. The treaty represented a great victory, but it left British finances exhausted. More expenses lay ahead: the new North American territories would have to be policed by troops to protect both the settlers and the Indians like Ontassetè, who were also subjects of King George—and dependable suppliers of furs. The solution was to tax the Americans. The war had benefited the empire and the Americans were part of the empire. They should help pay for their protection. As Parliament saw it, the reasoning was flawless and a law requiring government stamps to be placed on all publications and legal documents—the Stamp Act—was the result. But did the English Parliament have the right to levy internal taxes on the colonials, who had their own legislatures? If it did, it had never exercised the right before.

At first, even in America nobody made much of the question. When news of the impending tax reached

resembled the scene shown in this painting, titled Colonial Wedding in Virginia.

the colonies many people grumbled mildly but solid citizens—later to become patriots—applied for posts as stampsellers. Virginia's House of Burgesses sent off messages to the King, the Lords, and Commons, "praying," as Fauquier put it, "to be permitted to tax themselves."

When London failed to answer the appeals, most Americans felt nothing more remained to be done. In the May, 1765 session of the Burgesses, a new member, Patrick Henry, fumed at the weakness of his older, more dignified colleagues.

The session was almost over. Two-thirds of the members had gone home. Patrick Henry tore a blank page from an old law book and with the aid of an able lawyer named George Johnson, wrote hot-worded resolutions, containing the declaration that the "sole right and power to levy taxes and impositions upon the inhabitants of this colony" belonged to the colonials' elected representatives.

The debate that followed was "bloody," Jefferson relates. He and his friend John Tyler, both still studying law, stood listening in the assembly's lobby that Thursday, May 29, 1765. The opposition, which included Wythe, Peyton Randolph, and the distinguished lawyer Edmund Pendleton—argued that Henry's

The Forest, where Jefferson was married.

angry resolutions merely restated points already made in a more tactful manner.

Henry made an eloquent reply. It was hard to tell, later, just what he had said, but Jefferson thought that he spoke "as Homer wrote." And at one point—as Jefferson and Tyler remembered it half a century later—he cried: "Caesar had his Brutus, Charles the First his Cromwell, and George the Third . . . "

"Treason!" warned Speaker John Robinson. "Treason! Treason!" echoed Wythe and other moderate men.

"And George the Third," Henry went on gracefully, "may profit by their example. If *this* be treason, make the most of it."

At first the Burgesses approved Henry's resolutions, but the next day, when Henry had ridden off to the backwoods, some of his supporters had repented their daring and the house reversed itself.

Signature of Martha Wayles Jefferson.

It did not matter. Anti-stamp riots erupted anyway. Stamps were burned. The less violent people simply refused to buy them. In Boston a mob wrecked the lieutenant governor's house.

Patrick Henry, who had given England one warning in the case of the ministers' pay, had now shaken the foundations of the Empire, shaken them so thoroughly that when Jefferson passed through Annapolis, New York-bound, some months later, he found the town celebrating: the King and his ministers had yielded and the Stamp Act had been repealed!

Something vastly important, but little realized at the time, had happened. The colonies had behaved almost like a family.

The quarrel smouldered and flickered for several years, and when Jefferson took his seat as a burgess in May, 1769, it was flaring again. The King's ministers had poked the fire: since the colonials would not accept an internal tax, the government imposed an external tax, a duty on goods the colonies imported. Import duties had been used, up to that time, only to regulate trade, not to raise revenue. The new plan infuriated the colonies. Massachusetts' legislature had written to the other colonial legislatures urging united action. Before Jefferson joined the House, the House had petitioned the King for repeal of the taxes, known as the Townshend duties.

Britain responded by ordering Massachusetts to take back what it had said in its letter. The colonial governors were ordered to dissolve any legislature that approved it; furthermore, Britain threatened to make use of an ancient and disused law to bring colonial "traitors"—such as the Massachusetts legislators—to London for trial and possible hanging.

The House answered by quietly insisting upon both its loyalty to the Crown and its exclusive right to levy taxes on the colony. And it warned that trial of a colonial in England would be fraught with "dangers and miseries."

The kindly Governor Botetourt, whose sympathies were with the colonials, carried out his orders. He summoned the Burgesses the next day, May 17, 1769, and, splendid in his red coat, dissolved them.

The members of the dissolved House continued their business in the Raleigh Tavern's elegant Apollo Room and next day Jefferson signed his first revolutionary document. It was an agreement—drawn by George Mason, brought from Fairfax County in the pocket of Mason's neighbor, George Washington, and adopted by eighty-nine former burgesses—not to buy a long list of British goods until the Townshend duties were repealed.

No punishment befell the defiant eighty-nine. Britain's exports dropped sharply and London businessmen put pressure on Parliament to lift the duties. Botetourt had to have a legislature. When he called new elections, all former burgesses were renamed, except the few who had ignored the boycott. At Jefferson's second session as a burgess, Botetourt was able to announce happily that the London government was going to remove the duties on a number of articles. But Jefferson and a few others were disturbed because Botetourt had said nothing about tea. The tea tax stood, a reminder from Britain of Britain's power. The tax had become a matter of principle.

To Jefferson too, the tea tax was a matter of principle and he continued to boycott imports—months after other men had tired. But rioting in New York in January, 1770, over billeting of British soldiers, and the Boston Massacre in March had made people cautious. When the Townshend duties were finally lifted in April—about the time Jefferson was trying to free Howell—few men wanted to keep the quarrel alive.

The September after their marriage, the Jeffersons became parents of a daughter, named Martha, and nicknamed Patsy. The housebuilding was progressing. Dabney Carr

The First Continental Congress met here, at the State House in Philadelphia, in 1774. This 1799 view shows a party of sightseeing Indians in the foreground.

was becoming an important lawyer and people said he was almost a match for Patrick Henry. He made a name for himself in the House of Burgesses when Jefferson asked him to introduce the idea of setting up a Committee of Correspondence in Virginia. This Committee was to keep similar committees in other colonies informed by mail of the ways citizens were protesting unfair British laws and taxes. In this way, the divided colonies might eventually act together. Carr's speech suggesting the formation of a committee was a great success, and Virginia soon set up its own Committee of Correspondence.

Soon after his triumph, Carr fell ill in Charlottesville and died on May 16, 1773. He was buried at Shadwell. When Jefferson returned from Williamsburg, he moved his friend to the spot beneath the hilltop oak, where they had read and talked and dreamed as boys. By the grave Jefferson set a stone, on which is carved under Carr's name: "To his Virtue, Good Sense, Learning and Friendship, this stone is dedicated by

Thomas Jefferson, who of all men living loved him most."

Mrs. Jefferson's father, John Wayles, died on May 28 in the same year. Jefferson's grief was not eased by the fact that his father-in-law's passing made him—temporarily—a much richer man.

Nobody could replace the departed friends, but Jefferson acquired a fascinating new one. This was the Tuscan, Philip Mazzei, who had practiced medicine in Turkey and diplomacy in London as ambassador of Tuscany's Grand Duke. He had come to America to grow wine grapes for Thomas Adams, from whom Jefferson had bought a piano for Martha. One November evening Adams brought Mazzei to Monticello. Jefferson, who wanted to practice his self-taught Italian, was disappointed that Mazzei spoke English, but they liked each other at once. Early next morning, Mazzei agreed to settle on 2,000 acres provided by Jefferson, and to try to grow grapes for wine and olives for oil. "I knew you would take him away from me," Adams ruefully remarked to Jefferson when the two new friends came back from a walk around the hilltop.

The British law closing the port of Boston on June 1, 1774, as punishment for the Boston Tea Party outraged Jefferson, Patrick Henry, the Lees, George Mason, and George Wythe. But how could they make *all* Virginians feel that Boston's trouble was their problem too? How could they get cautious, conservative citizens to do more than sputter a bit? Jefferson hit on an idea: he proposed that the House of Burgesses proclaim June 1 a day of fasting and prayer, and, cleverly, he got the pious Robert Carter Nicholas to introduce the resolution.

The House approved the scheme unanimously. Lord Dunmore, who had become Governor of Virginia on the death of Lord Botetcourt and had, as one of his first official acts, dissolved the House again. Moving over to the Raleigh once more, the Burgesses agreed that "an attack on any one colony should be considered as an attack on the whole." They agreed that the colonies ought to meet in an annual congress which could tackle common problems better than the Committees of Correspondence could. They called elections in Virginia to choose delegates to a convention on August 1 in Williamsburg. The convention would be outside the law so Dunmore could not dissolve it. The convention would pick Virginia's deputies to the proposed colonial congress.

Jefferson became ill on his way to the convention and had to return home, but he had written down some ideas to guide Virginia's deputies to the congress. He sent a copy to Patrick Henry, another to Peyton Randolph. "Whether Mr. Henry disapproved the ground taken," Jefferson said later, "or was too lazy to

A

SUMMARY VIEW

OF THE

RIGHTS

OF

BRITISH AMERICA.

SET FORTH IN SOME

RESOLUTIONS

INTENDED FOR THE

INSPECTION

OF THE PRESENT

DELEGATES

OF THE

PEOPLE OF VIRGINIA.

NOW IN

CONVENTION.

BY A NATIVE, AND MEMBER OF THE HOUSE OF BURGESSES.
by Thomas Jefferson

WILLIAMSBURG:
PRINTED BY CLEMENTINA RIND.

Title page of Jefferson's Summary View.

read it (for he was the laziest man in reading I ever knew) I never learned: but he communicated it to nobody." Randolph, on the other hand, dutifully passed his copy around among the delegates.

"Our Ancestors . . ." Jefferson had written, "possessed a right, which nature has given to all men, of departing from the country in which chance, not choice, has placed them, of going in quest of new habitations, and of there establishing new societies, under such laws . . . as to them, shall seem most likely to promote public happiness . . . America was conquered, and her settlements . . . established, at the expense of individuals, and not of the British public."

Jefferson felt that the relationship between America and England was like that of England and the German state of Hanover: they simply had the same King. But the King was "no more than the chief officer of the people . . . and . . . subject to their superintendence." Americans, he felt, had not submitted to England's Parliament. The convention found Jefferson's sentiments too strong and came to the Continental Congress on September 5 with milder suggestions for solving the colonies' problems. But Jefferson's paper somehow found its way into print as a pamphlet, with the title *A Summary View of the Rights of British America.* It created as great a commotion in England, where many people opposed the government's colonial practices, as it did in America. The First Continental Congress when it met in September 1774, initiated a boycott of British goods designed to alter Britain's attitude. Enforced with astonishing effectiveness, it only widened the breach. People were choosing between King and colony, and Jefferson's cousin John Randolph—Peyton Randolph's brother—chose to side with the King. Sadly, Jefferson sent him thirteen pounds for his violin before he left for England.

In the Spring, Jefferson, attending Virginia's convention, heard Patrick

Henry shake the rafters of Virginia's old Saint John's Church with his defiance: "Give me liberty or give me death." The words were echoing through the colonies when the farmers of Lexington and Concord took part in a skirmish with British troops on April 19, 1775, and "fired the shot heard 'round the world."

Too late, the King's chief minister, Lord North, made a proposal which he thought would win approval in the colonies; it had to be rejected because it maintained Parliament's right to interfere in colonial affairs. Peyton Randolph asked Jefferson to write the reply, in which Jefferson included the sharp words: "For us, not for them, has government been instituted here."

A company of riflemen in hunting shirts descended on Williamsburg. A burgess wanted to hang Lord Dunmore, who prudently joined his family on a British man-of-war, anchored in the James. The Burgesses,

In 1771, Jefferson made this sketch of the home he was planning: Monticello.

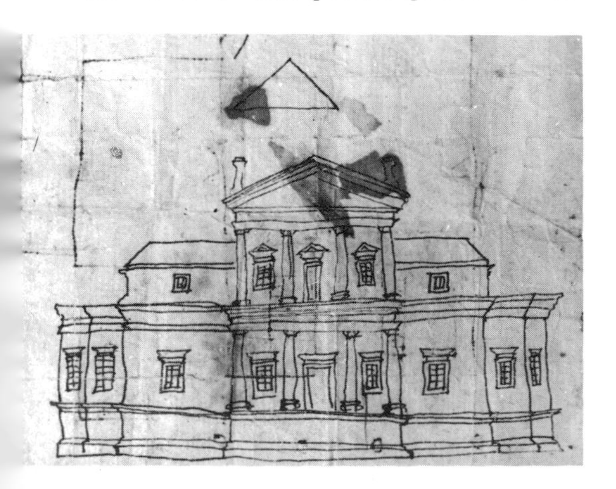

Jefferson at the age of 33, the year he wrote the Declaration of Independence.

with grim humor, protested his absence and adjourned June 21, 1775. And that was the end of the House of Burgesses.

Jefferson set out on June 11 for Philadelphia to sit in the Second Continental Congress as Peyton Randolph's alternate. Virginia's other delegates, Washington, Patrick Henry, Richard Henry Lee, Edmund Pendleton, Benjamin Harrison, and Richard Bland, were already there.

When he reached Philadelphia he stayed in the house of Benjamin Randolph, a cabinetmaker. He took his meals at the City Tavern, where George Washington left a vacant place at the table three days after Jefferson's arrival. News had come of the Battle of Bunker Hill on June 17, and Washington—newly elected commander of Continental forces—rode to Boston.

This late 18th-century view of Norfolk harbor was painted by Benjamin Latrobe. In January, 1776, Lord Dunmore attacked Norfolk by sea, and burned the town.

Only two men in Congress—John Jay and Edward Rutledge—were younger than Jefferson, but he was quickly asked to serve with the elderly Benjamin Franklin, John Adams, and Richard Henry Lee on a committee to write Congress' reply to Lord North. It was almost identical with Virginia's.

For Jefferson, the Congressional recess that followed was marked by sadness. Shortly after his return to Monticello his eighteen-month-old daughter, Jane Randolph Jefferson, died. Jefferson was deeply upset, but he remained calm: his country was in a state of undeclared war, and he had just been named commander of his county's militia.

When he did set out again for Philadelphia, he took along his servant Bob, and had him inoculated there against smallpox.

The colonies were torn apart with conflict. In Virginia, Lord Dunmore proclaimed martial law, offered to free any slaves who joined him, and bombarded and burned Norfolk, making homeless five or six thousand people, many of whom were loyal to Britain. Jefferson, worried about Martha and Patsy, from whom—mysteriously—he had had no word for weeks, went home and stayed four months. He was there when his mother died in March and he was there when a pamphlet called *Common Sense* arrived from Philadelphia. It had been written by Tom Paine, an Englishman who had moved to Philadelphia two years before. It proved to be one of the most influential pamphlets ever printed; in simple, stirring language, it demolished monarchism as a political philosophy and set up democracy in its place.

"O ye that love mankind," Paine wrote, "he that dare not only to oppose tyranny but the tyrant, stand forth! Every spot in the old world is overrun with oppression. The birthday of a new world is at hand!"

The quarrel between the Mother Country, headed by the King, and the colonies had begun over internal taxes. At first it seemed like an almost private fight between the government, represented by the King, and a few hotheaded men, like Patrick Henry of Virginia and Samuel Adams of Massachusetts. But the British government behaved so cynically or so clumsily that they produced sober recruits for the side of the revolutionaries. Every act issued by the King for his government which was intended to punish or discipline the colonies produced violent reactions in America. But Americans remained loyal to the Crown even after they had exchanged gunfire with Britons. They were ripe, though, for a break. Paine's pamphlet, of which there were 120,000 copies circulating, helped to make Americans think of themselves as republicans.

The revolutionary cause was furthered by the British and by some new help from the French. The British had evacuated besieged Boston and were attacking Charleston, South Carolina. The French, delighted at their ancient enemy's troubles, decided to give gunpowder and guns secretly to the Americans.

One day in mid-May, the bells of Williamsburg's Bruton Church began ringing. The British flag descended abruptly from the pole on the State House. A thirteen-striped banner with a Union Jack at the upper left was raised.

Jefferson wrote later, "On the 15th of May, 1776, the Convention of Virginia instructed their delegates in Congress to propose to that body to declare the colonies independent of Great Britain and appointed a committee to prepare a declaration of rights and a plan of government." From that day Virginia considered herself independent.

When the church bells rang in Williamsburg, Jefferson was not there. With his servant Bob, and carrying contributions of cash to buy powder for Virginians and food for Bostonians, he had set out again on May 7 for Philadelphia.

On Friday, June 7, 1776, Richard Henry Lee introduced in Congress a resolution carrying out the instructions from home. It resolved:

"That these United Colonies are & of right ought to be free & independent states, that they are absolved from all allegiance to the British Crown, and that all political con-

In CONGRESS, July 4, 1776.

The unanimous Declaration of the thirteen united States of America,

When in the Course of human events, it becomes necessary for one people to dissolve the political bands which have connected them with another, and to assume among the powers of the earth, the separate and equal station to which the Laws of Nature and of Nature's God entitle them, a decent respect to the opinions of mankind requires that they should declare the causes which impel them to the separation. —— We hold these truths to be self-evident, that all men are created equal, that they are endowed by their Creator with certain unalienable Rights, that among these are Life, Liberty and the pursuit of Happiness. — That to secure these rights, Governments are instituted among Men, deriving their just powers from the consent of the governed, — That whenever any Form of Government becomes destructive of these ends, it is the Right of the People to alter or to abolish it, and to institute new Government, laying its foundation on such principles and organizing its powers in such form, as to them shall seem most likely to effect their Safety and Happiness. Prudence, indeed, will dictate that Governments long established should not be changed for light and transient causes; and accordingly all experience hath shewn, that mankind are more disposed to suffer, while evils are sufferable, than to right themselves by abolishing the forms to which they are accustomed. But when a long train of abuses and usurpations, pursuing invariably the same Object evinces a design to reduce them under absolute Despotism, it is their right, it is their duty, to throw off such Government, and to provide new Guards for their future security. — Such has been the patient sufferance of these Colonies; and such is now the necessity which constrains them to alter their former Systems of Government. The history of the present King of Great Britain is a history of repeated injuries and usurpations, all having in direct object the establishment of an absolute Tyranny over these States. To prove this, let Facts be submitted to a candid world. —— He has refused his Assent to Laws, the most wholesome and necessary for the public good. —— He has forbidden his Governors to pass Laws of immediate and pressing importance, unless suspended in their operation till his Assent should be obtained; and when so suspended, he has utterly neglected to attend to them. —— He has refused to pass other Laws for the accommodation of large districts of people, unless those people would relinquish the right of Representation in the Legislature, a right inestimable to them and formidable to tyrants only. —— He has called together legislative bodies at places unusual, uncomfortable, and distant from the depository of their Public Records, for the sole purpose of fatiguing them into compliance with his measures. —— He has dissolved Representative Houses repeatedly, for opposing with manly firmness his invasions on the rights of the people. —— He has refused for a long time, after such dissolutions, to cause others to be elected; whereby the Legislative powers, incapable of Annihilation, have returned to the People at large for their exercise; the State remaining in the mean time exposed to all the dangers of invasion from without, and convulsions within. —— He has endeavoured to prevent the population of these States; for that purpose obstructing the Laws for Naturalization of Foreigners; refusing to pass others to encourage their migrations hither, and raising the conditions of new Appropriations of Lands. —— He has obstructed the Administration of Justice, by refusing his Assent to Laws for establishing Judiciary powers. —— He has made Judges dependent on his Will alone, for the tenure of their offices, and the amount and payment of their salaries. —— He has erected a multitude of New Offices, and sent hither swarms of Officers to harrass our people, and eat out their substance. —— He has kept among us, in times of peace, Standing Armies without the Consent of our legislatures. —— He has affected to render the Military independent of and superior to the Civil power. —— He has combined with others to subject us to a jurisdiction foreign to our constitution, and unacknowledged by our laws; giving his Assent to their Acts of pretended Legislation: — For Quartering large bodies of armed troops among us: — For protecting them, by a mock Trial, from punishment for any Murders which they should commit on the Inhabitants of these States: — For cutting off our Trade with all parts of the world: — For imposing Taxes on us without our Consent: — For depriving us in many cases, of the benefits of Trial by Jury: — For transporting us beyond Seas to be tried for pretended offences — For abolishing the free System of English Laws in a neighbouring Province, establishing therein an Arbitrary government, and enlarging its Boundaries so as to render it at once an example and fit instrument for introducing the same absolute rule into these Colonies: — For taking away our Charters, abolishing our most valuable Laws, and altering fundamentally the Forms of our Governments: — For suspending our own Legislatures, and declaring themselves invested with power to legislate for us in all cases whatsoever. — He has abdicated Government here, by declaring us out of his Protection and waging War against us. —— He has plundered our seas, ravaged our Coasts, burnt our towns, and destroyed the lives of our people. —— He is at this time transporting large Armies of foreign Mercenaries to compleat the works of death, desolation and tyranny, already begun with circumstances of Cruelty & perfidy scarcely paralleled in the most barbarous ages, and totally unworthy the Head of a civilized nation. —— He has constrained our fellow Citizens taken Captive on the high Seas to bear Arms against their Country, to become the executioners of their friends and Brethren, or to fall themselves by their Hands. —— He has excited domestic insurrections amongst us, and has endeavoured to bring on the inhabitants of our frontiers, the merciless Indian Savages, whose known rule of warfare, is an undistinguished destruction of all ages, sexes and conditions. In every stage of these Oppressions We have Petitioned for Redress in the most humble terms: Our repeated Petitions have been answered only by repeated injury. A Prince, whose character is thus marked by every act which may define a Tyrant, is unfit to be the ruler of a free people. Nor have We been wanting in attentions to our Brittish brethren. We have warned them from time to time of attempts by their legislature to extend an unwarrantable jurisdiction over us. We have reminded them of the circumstances of our emigration and settlement here. We have appealed to their native justice and magnanimity, and we have conjured them by the ties of our common kindred to disavow these usurpations, which, would inevitably interrupt our connections and correspondence. They too have been deaf to the voice of justice and of consanguinity. We must, therefore, acquiesce in the necessity, which denounces our Separation, and hold them, as we hold the rest of mankind, Enemies in War, in Peace Friends. ——

We, therefore, the Representatives of the united States of America, in General Congress, Assembled, appealing to the Supreme Judge of the world for the rectitude of our intentions, do, in the Name, and by Authority of the good People of these Colonies, solemnly publish and declare, That these United Colonies are, and of Right ought to be Free and Independent States; that they are Absolved from all Allegiance to the British Crown, and that all political connection between them and the State of Great Britain, is and ought to be totally dissolved; and that as Free and Independent States, they have full Power to levy War, conclude Peace, contract Alliances, establish Commerce, and to do all other Acts and Things which Independent States may of right do. —— And for the support of this Declaration, with a firm reliance on the protection of divine Providence, we mutually pledge to each other our Lives, our Fortunes and our sacred Honor.

John Hancock

Button Gwinnett
Lyman Hall
Geo Walton.
Wm Hooper
Joseph Hewes,
John Penn
Edward Rutledge 1.
Thos Heyward Junr.
Thomas Lynch Junr.
Arthur Middleton
Samuel Chase
Wm Paca
Thos Stone
Charles Carroll of Carrollton
George Wythe
Richard Henry Lee
Th Jefferson
Benj Harrison
Thos Nelson jr.
Francis Lightfoot Lee
Carter Braxton
Robt Morris
Benjamin Rush
Benja. Franklin
John Morton
Geo Clymer
Jas. Smith.
Geo. Taylor
James Wilson
Geo. Ross
Caesar Rodney
Geo Read
Thos M:Kean
Wm Floyd
Phil. Livingston
Frans. Lewis
Lewis Morris
Richd. Stockton
Jno Witherspoon
Fras. Hopkinson
John Hart
Abra Clark
Josiah Bartlett
Wm Whipple
Saml Adams
John Adams
Robt Treat Paine
Elbridge Gerry
Step. Hopkins
William Ellery
Roger Sherman
Saml Huntington
Wm Williams
Oliver Wolcott
Matthew Thornton

On this facsimile of the Declaration of Independence, Jefferson's signature is eighth below that of John Hancock. It is not widely known that Jefferson originally condemned the slave trade in the Declaration, because all his fiery remarks on the subject were removed from the text before Congress approved it on July 4, 1776. But the noble words that Jefferson wrote in it (. . . "We hold these truths to be self evident: that all men are created equal; that they are endowed by their Creator with certain inalienable rights; that among these are life, liberty and the pursuit of happiness . . .") are words Americans will never forget.

nection between them & the state of Great Britain is & ought to be, totally dissolved."

When the hurricane of debate died down a bit the following Tuesday, a vote on the resolution was set for July 1, and a committee appointed to draft a declaration of independence. It consisted of John Adams of Massachusetts, Benjamin Franklin of Pennsylvania, Roger Sherman of Connecticut, Robert R. Livingston of New York, and Thomas Jefferson of Virginia.

Jefferson was chosen to put the ideas of the Committee into writing. John Adams recalled that on visiting Jefferson after he had started work on the Declaration, Jefferson suggested that Adams, an older member of the Committee, write the document. Adams replied, "I am feared and hated in Congress." He capped his argument with a frank statement, "You write ten times better than I do."

So for seventeen days, from June 11 to June 28, Jefferson toiled at his writing desk in the second floor parlor. He drew from his encyclopedic memory, from his own earlier writings, and from the Declaration of Rights which George Mason had written for Virginia.

". . . Not to find out new principles, or new arguments, never before thought of, not merely to say things which had never been said before; but to place before mankind the common sense of the subject, in terms so plain and firm as to command their assent, and to justify ourselves in the independent stand we are compelled to take."

Jefferson turned the Declaration over to the Convention on June 28. The Convention made only minor changes. Debate was shortened by the heat and the horseflies that buzzed into Carpenter's Hall from a nearby livery stable, stinging the delegates through their silk stockings. On July 2, Congress approved the Declaration and next day tackled Richard Henry Lee's independence resolution.

On July 4, Mr. Jefferson rose at daybreak as usual, and soaked his feet in chill water, a lifelong custom to which he credited his freedom from colds. At 6 A.M. he noted in his *Account Book* that the temperature stood at 68 degrees. It was just another day. But in the evening twelve of the states—New York hung back a few days—approved Lee's independence resolution.

Philadelphia did some celebrating on July 8. Troops paraded and bells rang. Jefferson did not get a chance to sign his own Declaration until August 2. The signers' names were not even made public, officially, until January, 1777.

Mr. Jefferson, the lanky thirty-three-year-old who had failed a few years before to free Samuel Howell, had added a great accomplishment to the clearing of the Rivanna: he had helped to free a nation.

In Carpenter's Hall, Philadelphia, the Declaration of Independence was submitted to Congress on July 2, 1776. Two days later, on July 4, it was accepted.

The drafting committee, including John Adams, Roger Sherman, Robert Livingston, Thomas Jefferson, and Benjamin Franklin, stands at the speaker's desk.

Edmund Pendleton, a leading conservative, helped Jefferson and George Wythe revise Virginia's state laws in 1779.

JEFFERSON THE LEGISLATOR (1776-1779)

In a committee of Virginia's House of Delegates, Jefferson and his distinguished old friend Edmund Pendleton were arguing.

Jefferson wanted to change an ancient law which gave the eldest son the whole family fortune in the absence of a will. Aware that he was losing, but yielding as little ground as possible, Pendleton suggested: "At least let us keep by the old biblical law and let the oldest son have twice as much as the rest."

With his habitual deceptive mildness and a smile, Jefferson replied that if the eldest son could eat twice as much or do twice as much work as the others he would agree. Otherwise, no.

Jefferson wanted to change many things in his new state. Virginia as a state differed from Virginia the colony chiefly in that Patrick Henry was governor instead of Dunmore. Colonial Virginia had been virtually a rural English county dominated by rich landowners, elegant in periwigs and silken breeches. Independent Virginia was a republic dominated by rich landowners in periwigs and silken breeches.

No law had been altered by a comma. Virginia had inherited many old-fashioned laws from England—some of them not even enforced any longer in the Mother Country—which limited the liberty and safety of the individual man. There were many harsh laws which limited the religious freedom of men not belonging to the established Church of England. Witches and heretics could still be burned at the stake. And perhaps most disturbing of all to Jefferson were the laws permitting and governing the slave trade and the holding of slaves.

Few men in the newly freed colonies realized as Jefferson did, that it would take more than a Declaration of Independence and a bloody campaign to establish real freedom; that there was more to the Revolution

Jefferson could not abolish slavery and slave auctions, like this one. But in 1778, he had Virginia pass a law which prevented the importing of more slaves.

than replacing the King's governor with a less disagreeable fellow.

So while he sat with Congress in Philadelphia in the late spring and summer of 1776, where John Hancock was presiding over the Congress' endless debating, and when he was not tackling the scores of chores that his "country" passed on to him, Jefferson worked away at his portable desk.

The document he sent to Williamsburg, "on the mere possibility that it might suggest something" worth putting into the Constitution, provided absolute freedom of religion and of the press. It barred import of slaves. It ended the death penalty except for murder or military offenses. It gave all children—even girls—equal rights of inheritance. It provided for three governmental branches—executive, judicial, and legislative. And since only landowners could vote, it provided that the government would give landless men up to fifty acres, purchased from the Indians.

Some of the ideas might have had a fighting chance, but the plan reached Williamsburg when the delegates were too weary to reopen the argument they had just concluded.

Jefferson believed someone else should enjoy a chance to sit in Congress, and he had decided not to stay after his term expired in August. The Williamsburg convention re-elected him anyway, but when he saw the new Virginia Constitution—which embodied George Mason's

For timing astronomical observations, Jefferson ordered a copy of this clock from Rittenhouse.

Declaration of Rights and really was not as bad as Jefferson thought—he was certain his place was in the new House of Delegates.

Jefferson could not get away from Philadelphia until September, and had been home only a few weeks when a tempting offer arrived from John Hancock. Congress wanted Jefferson to go to France with Benjamin Franklin and Silas Deane to negotiate treaties. For three days Jefferson kept the courier waiting. His final, reluctant "No," explained that his wife was too ill to travel. He would not go without her.

Jefferson devoted his full energies to Virginia. "Our revolution presented to us an album on which we were free to write what we pleased," Jefferson once said. When he took his seat in the House of Delegates on October 7, 1776, he knew what he wanted to write in the album.

Jefferson's most important idea was this: If the country were divided between a few people who owned much land, and a great many people who owned little or no land, trouble was certain. If industry developed, and Jefferson hoped it would not, the landless people would crowd the cities. Once in the cities they might become the raw material of mobs as had happened in Europe.

But if everyone were to receive as much land as he could farm without slaves—probably fifty acres—the country would develop self-reliant citizens, determined to defend their soil and the freedom they enjoyed upon it.

There was land enough. But there were obstacles, specifically a couple of feudal English laws. Even the English had changed them. But in Virginia they retained their ancient shape. One, called entail, or fee tail, allowed a landowner to say that his acres must never be divided, even after he had been dead for centuries. The other, called primogeniture (from the Latin *primus*, first, and *genitura*, birth) gave the eldest son everything if his father died without writing a will. If the property that the eldest son inherited was entailed, he could not share it with his younger brothers and sisters.

Rittenhouse's orrery—a device which indicated the motions of the planets of the Solar System—fascinated Jefferson.

Jefferson feared that the perpetually rich families would gobble the western lands, and the small farmers on whom he was basing his hopes would have no place to go.

Five days after the House met, Jefferson introduced a bill to abolish entail. It met opposition but just eleven days after he launched his attack on it, centuries-old entail was abolished. Primogeniture went later.

Jefferson did not think that merely giving a man land would make him wise. He believed in aristocracy (from the Greek *aristos*, best, and *kratein*, to rule) but he believed in a natural aristocracy of "virtue and talents" rather than one of inherited wealth and privilege. "That form of government is best," he told John Adams, "which provides the most effectually for a pure selection of these natural *aristoi* into the offices of government."

A theodolite, like this one, was used by Jefferson for his surveying.

Jefferson's friend David Rittenhouse was a clockmaker who made precision instruments. His clock and orrery appear here.

To accomplish this "pure selection" Jefferson proposed an ingenious school system. He planned to divide every county into districts six miles square, with a school for each district and a hundred children to a school. Each child would get three years of reading, writing, and arithmetic, free. That would be enough for most, but they could continue if their parents paid.

Every year each school would select its brightest poor boy and send him, free, to one of twenty boarding schools. Each year the boarding school would weed out all but the top of the class; if you were really good, you might last at boarding school—which Jefferson called grammar school—for six years. At the end of six years, half of the survivors would be sent home—probably, Jefferson thought, to become school teachers. The brighter half would go on to study for three years, still free, at William and Mary.

Courageously and with splendid logic, he tackled the religious laws. A man was accountable for his beliefs, said Jefferson, only to his God. They were none of the government's business and whenever in the past government and religion had been allied, only tyranny had been served. In writing about religious toleration, Jefferson wrote:

> "Reason and persuasion are the only practicable instruments. To make way for these, free inquiry must be indulged; and how can we wish others to indulge it while we refuse it ourselves?"

Slavery presented an even tougher challenge. Jefferson thought it to be as bad for master as for slaves. He never bought a slave himself, but he had acquired approximately 150 by inheritance and marriage. He did not free them because the practice "as far as I can judge from the experiments . . . made to give liberty, or rather, to abandon persons whose habits have been formed in slavery, is like abandoning children."

So he evolved an elaborate plan: The children of slaves would be born free. They would be educated at state expense. When grown, they would be settled in communities of their own, where they would not be constantly reminded of slavery. Free immigrants from Europe would take over negroes' work in Virginia.

Another problem was presented by the very language of the laws. In the jumble of statutes inherited from England were many written before the Magna Carta. Because of the great changes in English, they were difficult to read. They were also difficult to understand; they even confused good lawyers. Jefferson suggested that somebody capable of writing clearly revise all of Virginia's laws, striking out the useless and the barbaric phrases, and writing the remainder in simple English. Wythe, Pendleton, and Jefferson got the job. When they finished several years later, they had reduced the long shelves of dusty English lawbooks to 126 clear, concise bills that filled only ninety printed pages.

Jefferson managed to eliminate quickly the worst religious laws, and some of the most barbarous punishments for crimes. He got the death penalty restricted to murder and treason and he made it easy for immigrants to become citizens.

The slave emancipation plan got nowhere. The plantations in Virginia were prosperous and not many people wanted to change the system which they felt had made the prosperity possible. Jefferson's school system was adopted in part in 1796 but was never put into full operation.

Jefferson's days as a delegate were not given over to debate in Wil-

A modern painting shows British Lt. Col. Henry Hamilton (the "Hair Buyer") surrendering Ft. Sackville, at Vincennes, to George Rogers Clark in February, 1779.

liamsburg, or to the chore of revising dusty laws and fashioning bright new ones at home in Monticello. He recorded the planting of the purple cabbage, the peas, the strawberries. He noted on April 1: "Peach trees & Cherry trees at Monticello begin to blossom." He acquired from Mazzei an olive tree and four sour orange trees and received sound instruction on how to plant and care for them.

Martha presented him with his first and only son on May 28, 1777, and he was plunged into grief when the boy died after three weeks. But a little sister for Patsy arrived August 1, 1778, and was named Mary and nicknamed Polly.

He delved into astronomy as well as meteorology and optics. When he almost missed an eclipse of the sun on June 26, 1778—the first one ever carefully observed on this continent—because his instruments were inadequate, he asked the learned David Rittenhouse of the Philosophical Society in Philadelphia about an astronomical clock which would prevent such mischances. He also discussed Rittenhouse's *orrery*, a kind of planetarium showing the positions and movement of bodies in the solar system.

Far to the west, about where Louisville, Kentucky, now stands, a little group of some of the bravest men on the frontier shot the "Falls of the Ohio" in the blackness of the eclipse that Jefferson almost missed. The men shooting the falls did not know the reason for their mission but Jefferson did—he had been involved with Governor Patrick Henry and a couple of other members of the House of Delegates in secret preparations for it.

The frontiersmen were led by a remarkable young man named George Rogers Clark. He had been born on a farm next to one of Peter Jefferson's. At 21, he had fought in Lord Dunmore's war against the Indians, and as a frontiersman he ranked with Daniel Boone. Clark, at 24, saw from the first what many American generals and statesmen did not: the new states might win every campaign against the British in the east and yet lose the war by failing to gain the west.

Settlers had poured through the Cumberland Gap into Kentucky and had spread over the Alleghany and Monongahela valleys and along the Ohio. The newcomers cut down the forests to plant farms. The game fled. The dispossessed Indians launched desperate attacks on the

George Rogers Clark and his backwoodsmen firing on the fort at Vincennes.

intruders, who took refuge when they could in scattered blockhouses.

The French had built fortified settlements at Detroit, at Vincennes on the Wabash, at Kaskaskia and Cahokia along the Mississippi, among other places, but the French knew how to get along with the Indians. The French bought the Indians' furs, they often married Indian girls, and they did not cut down the forests as the British settlers had done.

When the British took over the forts, they installed British commanders and a few British soldiers, and kept on the Frenchmen to augment the garrisons.

The British commander at Detroit was a strange, brave, cruel, and unscrupulous soldier named Henry Hamilton who was called the "Hair Buyer" because he was supposed to pay the Indians for American scalps. In the winter of 1776–1777, he called together from far and wide the Sioux, the Chippewas, the Sauks and Foxes, the Winnebagoes, the Potawatomis, and the Menominees for a council of war.

A cultured man, he sang the Indians' wild songs, danced their firelit dances, and threw the hatchet with exquisite skill at a blood-smeared post hung with American frontiersmen's scalps. Hamilton stirred the Indians to war.

Clark came to Virginia to consult Patrick Henry on a scheme to capture the British posts northwest of the Ohio and eliminate the danger

George Rogers Clark

to settlers. Only Patrick Henry, Jefferson, Mason, and perhaps one or two others knew of the scheme. It was May, 1778, before he got 175 men and set out.

In the fantastic adventures that followed, Clark captured Kaskaskia by surprise. Then he led a starving handful of heroes for days through shoulder-deep, bitterly cold water—with the drummer boy riding dry astride a tall man—to swoop down on Vincennes. They took it too by surprise and captured Lieutenant Colonel Hamilton.

Clark's exploits undoubtedly hastened the war's end. They played a tremendous part in preparing for the opening of the west to Jefferson's future farmers. But unwittingly, by capturing Hamilton, Clark presented his old neighbor Jefferson with a bothersome problem when Jefferson became governor of Virginia in 1779.

The first governor of Virginia, after independence was declared, was Patrick Henry; the second was Thomas Jefferson. The royal arms were taken down, and a new emblem (above) designed, which showed Virtue trampling fallen Tyranny.

THE GOVERNOR OF VIRGINIA

(1779-1781)

In plumed hat and scarlet coat, Captain Jack Jouett looked a dashing fellow astride Prince Charley. Prince Charley was the fastest, toughest horse in seven counties, and he had to be, for Captain Jack was taller even than Governor Jefferson and weighed more than 200 pounds.

This is a silhouette of the huge (6′ 4″) Captain of the Virginia Militia, Jack Jouett, who warned Jefferson that Tarleton and his cavalry were approaching, on June 4, 1781.

But that pleasant spring Sunday evening—it was June 3, 1781—there seemed to be no particular test for their mettle, and they were staying at the Cuckoo Tavern, in the hamlet of Louisa, Virginia.

Along toward 11 P.M., Jouett peered out the window to identify the horsemen coming agallop. They were headed west, and Jack Jouett needed merely to glimpse their white coats to guess what was happening. Only Charlottesville, some forty miles away, lay between Louisa and the Blue Ridge. The House of Delegates was meeting there, and Governor Jefferson was home at Monticello. To the east Lord Cornwallis' troops were roaming over Virginia pretty much where they pleased. The white-coated cavalrymen—White Dragoons of Cornwallis' army—must be riding to surprise and capture the Governor and the legislators. Could warning be given in time?

Jouett knew his horse. And both knew wild, secret mountain paths.

Cornwallis' men, under the romantic, notorious Colonel Banastre Tarleton, rode seventy miles in twenty-four hours, traveling only by dark. Jouett and Prince Charley made their journey in five and one-half hours. At 4:30 A.M., hoofbeats awakened Jefferson. In the dawnlight, from the east portico, he perceived the massive figure riding to the step to be that of Jack Jouett, son of the man who kept Charlottesville's Swan Tavern. The sweat-streaked dust could not conceal the welts where vines and branches had lashed both the horse and his rider. Jack Jouett was scarred from the welts for the rest of his life.

Jefferson thanked Captain Jouett for his warning and then Jouett and Prince Charley raced down to Charlottesville to warn the legislators who were staying there. The Jeffersons and their house guests—some of the lawmakers were at Monticello—breakfasted in leisurely fashion. After breakfast, Jefferson sent Martha and the children off in a carriage via Blenheim to Enniscorthy, the fourteen-miles-distant estate of his friend Colonel Coles. The legislators went down to Charlottesville, met hastily, adjourned, and headed

Several of Tarleton's cavalrymen are seen in this skirmish which took place in South Carolina, just after the battle of Cowpens, in January, 1781.

home. One, General Edward Stevens, disguised himself as a farmer. He got away safely but seven others were captured.

Calmly, Jefferson burned some papers, set others aside to take with him. He spent two hours thus. Soon after Jouett's arrival, he had sent his best horse down to Shadwell for shoes. Jefferson went outside with his telescope and perched on a rock—where he had a fine view of Charlottesville—to see if the British had got there yet, and saw no sign of them.

He had time. He was striding back to Monticello to sort more papers when he noticed his small sword had fallen from its sheath, probably when he knelt on the rock. He went back. The sword was there. He took another look through the telescope. Charlottesville was alive with British: Tarleton's party numbered 180 White Dragoons and seventy mounted infantrymen.

Jefferson did not know that Tarleton had split his force in two, and that a detachment under a Captain McLeod was already near Monticello. Christopher Hudson, a young American officer who lived nearby, arrived to warn of immediate danger. He found Jefferson "perfectly tranquil and undisturbed."

A few minutes after Jefferson had left the house, the British thundered up. Two servants, Martin and Caesar, were hiding the silverware. Caesar was in a hole under the front portico's planks, and Martin was handing the valuables down to him. As the dragoons galloped up, Martin dumped the treasure down the hole and dropped the planks back in place over Caesar's head.

In 1779, this prison in Charlottesville, Virginia, received 4,000 of the British and German soldiers Burgoyne surrendered at Saratoga. Later that year, wartime Governor Jefferson had difficulty trying to find enough food for the prisoners.

At McLeod's command, Martin sullenly took the Britisher to tour the house. In the study, some of Jefferson's papers remained. McLeod locked the door from the outside and told Martin: "If anyone asks you for the key, tell him I have it." Then he gave the key to Martin. Not all British officers were Henry Hamiltons.

Out of McLeod's sight, a soldier, drunk on Jefferson's wine, held a pistol to Martin's head. "Tell me which way your master is gone or I fire," he demanded. Martin considered Jefferson his personal property. "Fire away," he dared the soldier. The soldier did not fire.

Having touched nothing but the wine, McLeod and his men finally rode off, and Caesar clambered out of the hole. He had remained motionless, without food and water, for eighteen hours.

Jefferson safely rejoined his family. Monticello, by Tarleton's orders, remained undamaged. Cornwallis was less a gentleman than his subordinate. Occupying another Jefferson plantation, Elkhill, Cornwallis destroyed the corn and tobacco crops, burned the barns and fences, cut the throats of horses too young to be pressed into British service, and carried off thirty slaves. "Had this been to give them freedom," said Jefferson, "he would have done right; but it was to consign them to inevitable death from the smallpox and putrid fever, then raging in his camp. This I knew afterwards to be the fate of twenty-seven of them."

Two and a half years earlier, shortly before Jefferson had become governor, the war had barely touched Virginia physically (except for isolated incidents like the burning of Norfolk). Jefferson was still rewriting the laws when Monticello's quiet was broken in January, 1779, by news of the arrival of 4,000 English and Hessian prisoners surrendered by Burgoyne at Saratoga.

They had been marched nearly seven hundred miles to the north bank of Ivy Creek, a few miles northwest of Charlottesville. The weather that met them was peculiar: hot from early February to mid-March,

Jefferson had little time to enjoy the gardens at the Governor's Palace in Williamsburg, for the capital moved to Richmond, for military reasons, in April, 1780. The Palace was an American military hospital during the Yorktown campaign.

followed by a killing frost and snowfall in the Blue Ridge.

Their barracks were unfinished. Their meat spoiled quickly for lack of salt. The prisoners were a miserable bunch at first and the question of moving them arose.

Investigating, Jefferson found the barracks completed, vegetable gardens thriving, and the prisoners hopeful of not being shifted. They had put much money and toil into making their camp comfortable.

Urging Governor Henry to let them be, Jefferson wrote: "Is an enemy so execrable, that, though in captivity, his wishes and comforts are to be disregarded and even crossed? I think not. It is for the benefit of mankind to mitigate the horrors of war as much as possible."

The prisoners and the Jeffersons became good friends. The Hessian Major General, Baron de Riedesel, rented Colle, the house of Philip Mazzei, who was departing on a secret mission for Virginia. Soon the baron's robust, bouncy, loud-singing wife, who shocked Virginians by riding in boots, was dropping in frequently on Martha, and the general's three young daughters were calling on Patsy and baby Polly. The Captain Baron de Geismar played the fiddle at Monticello, and when Jefferson helped to get him exchanged, he gave his host all his music.

New, desperately heavy responsibility soon was to end Jefferson's brief rest. Patrick Henry had served three single-year terms as governor. He could not legally be re-elected when his time was up on June 1 and the Assembly had to find a new governor. Jefferson and his old friends John Page and Thomas Nelson, Jr., were the only candidates anybody considered. The three were embarrassed to find themselves in competition, and none of them did anything to win. Jefferson was chosen.

It was a poor time to be governor. Soon after Jefferson, Martha, and the children moved into the Williamsburg Palace, Jefferson's first serious problem arose.

George Rogers Clark, having captured Henry Hamilton at Vincennes, sent him east in handcuffs with another captive, Captain William Lamothe.

Jefferson knew about Hamilton's habit of "buying" the scalps of other men from the Indians, so he and his council decided to keep Hamilton and Lamothe in irons, in a dungeon, without pen, ink, or paper; and without anybody to talk to except their keeper. Washington approved at first, but later relented, under British threats of reprisals. Finally, in October, 1780, Jefferson set Hamilton free, hoping his release would ease British treatment of Virginia prisoners. While it lasted, it was a nasty problem, but worse ones beset Jefferson.

In May, Henry's last month in office, a British naval expedition under Admiral Collier had captured Portsmouth and sent out raiding parties. At Suffolk, the major military depot, one such band routed 2,000 Virginia militiamen, which was not surprising since Virginia owned a single gun for every five militiamen and had little powder.

The plunderers destroyed large amounts of food that Virginia

In 1779, Jefferson sketched this floor plan of the main building of the Palace.

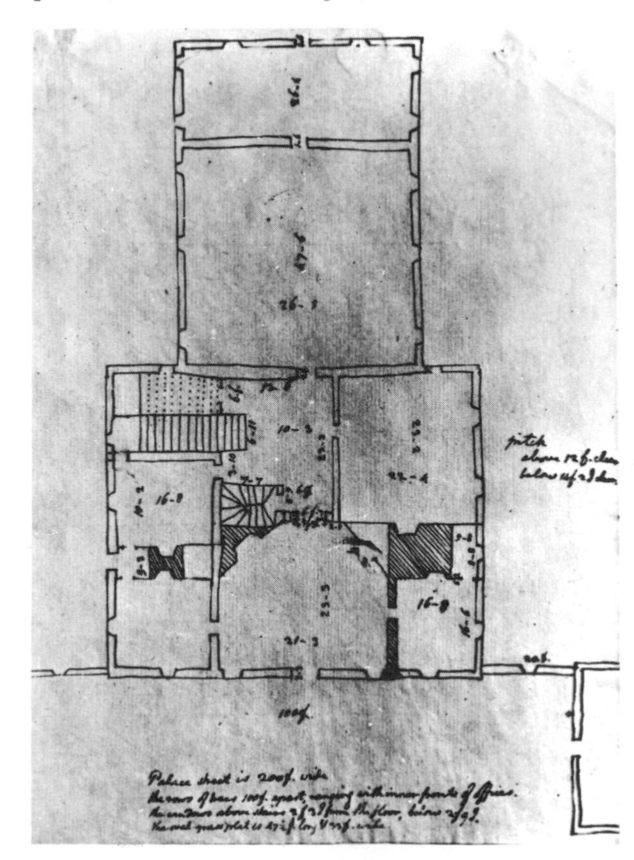

In September, 1781, Washington and Rochambeau marched their allied American and French troops to Virginia to begin the siege of Yorktown. This contemporary watercolor shows Rochambeau (mounted) at his Williamsburg headquarters.

could not afford to lose. The 1779 crops failed, partly because so many horses and so much manpower were in the army. Virginia had to import food, and the money to buy it was growing rapidly worthless.

Just before Jefferson became governor, the whole Continental army did not exceed 16,000 men. Washington pleaded constantly for more, but there were none to send. When the British turned their attention southward, to attack South Carolina, Washington had to detach Virginia's regulars for the state's defense, and most were captured when Charleston, S. C., surrendered on May 12, 1780. Jefferson, when he became

George Washington

James Monroe

governor, began to improve the role military intelligence played in winning and losing campaigns after the defeat. While discussing how to get information about troop movements from the front more efficiently, he met a young intelligence officer, James Monroe. Monroe's keen mind impressed Jefferson so much that he listened to what he had to say; and he also formed a friendship that was to last a lifetime.

More bad news came soon. Cornwallis and Tarleton roundly defeated General Horatio Gates at Camden, S. C., on August 16. Virginia militia, green and ill armed, behaved badly. All the desperately scarce supplies Virginia had scraped together for Gates had been lost.

Marquis de Lafayette

Virginia was open to invasion and Washington could spare no help. Wisely, Jefferson and the Assembly decided that Virginia could best defend herself by helping a neighbor. They set about scratching up more regulars and militia to assist North Carolina, and the men they eventually sent to Gates's successor, General Nathanael Greene, enabled him to undertake a campaign for South Carolina's liberation. They planned also to dispatch George Rogers Clark to take Detroit and forestall a British-Indian attack on Virginia's western borders in the spring.

Meanwhile, military intelligence from the south reached Jefferson late. He strung a line of couriers from the front to Richmond, which was now the capital. With a rider posted every forty miles, he hoped to speed the news 120 miles in twenty-four hours. To be his eyes and ears at the dangerous front end of the line, he picked a tall, serious, twenty-two-year-old named James Monroe, who had served Washington well as an officer, but was looking for a new assignment.

On Sunday, December 31, 1780, a fleet of twenty-seven warships sailed into Chesapeake Bay. Nobody yet knew whether they were British, bearing trouble, or French bringing help. On Tuesday, Jefferson learned they were British, ordered some of the militia mobilized, and made plans to move supplies out of enemy reach. Wednesday night, Jefferson

GENERAL ARNOLD.

Lord Cornwallis

got word the enemy was anchored off Jamestown. At 5 A.M. Thursday he summoned additional militia to defend Richmond and Petersburg.

He soon realized the capital would be indefensible and ordered arms, military supplies, and records moved five or six miles upriver to Westham. By late afternoon he learned that the British—some 1,600 infantry and cavalry under the American traitor Benedict Arnold—had landed north of the James at Westover, and were headed for Richmond. He had 200 men to oppose them. He stayed in the capital until 7:30 P.M., supervising the desperately hasty evacuation.

About one A.M. Friday, January 5, he galloped to Tuckahoe, where Martha had taken the children, and took them eight miles farther up the river, to stay at Fine Creek.

Then, in the rain and snow, he hastened toward Manchester, across the river from Richmond. He had been riding thirty-six hours and his horse fell exhausted. Jefferson pulled off the saddle, lugged it to a farmhouse, and put it on an unbroken colt.

From Manchester he could see the enemy enter Richmond. One British detachment rode off to Westham and destroyed the magazine and boring mill by fire. Jefferson was in Westham part of the time, but the British did not know it. He tried vainly to find Baron von Steuben, whom he had placed in command of the militia, and finally he rode off to see to his family.

Back in Manchester on Sunday, he saw the enemy retire from the capital, leaving nine unimportant buildings afire. Next day, Jefferson was back at work in Richmond.

Though Arnold had departed from the capital, Virginia's military situation was desperate and Jefferson's own affairs were in a tragic state. Cornwallis and Tarleton were seeping north. Arnold was pillaging almost at will to the east, and the Indians were harassing the west.

Jefferson's daughter Lucy Elizabeth, who had been born the previous November, died April 15.

Three days later, an 11-ship enemy fleet moved up the James. Arnold was back. But he did not get to Richmond this time. By forced march, Lafayette—who had been sent by Washington—arrived in the capital with his army on April 29. The young Frenchman had always wanted to meet Jefferson. Arnold retreated downriver.

But Richmond was not a safe capital. Cornwallis, Arnold, and General Phillips planned to join forces. It could be disastrous for Virginia, its military forces, and its government. That was why Jefferson was at Monticello and the Assembly had moved to Charlottesville when Jouett galloped over the mountain trails.

Legally, Jefferson was not even governor any more. His term had expired June 1, but the legislators had not been able to sit still long enough to choose a new one.

This map traces Arnold's raid on Richmond in January, 1781. The threat of more British raids forced Jefferson to move the capital to Charlottesville in May.

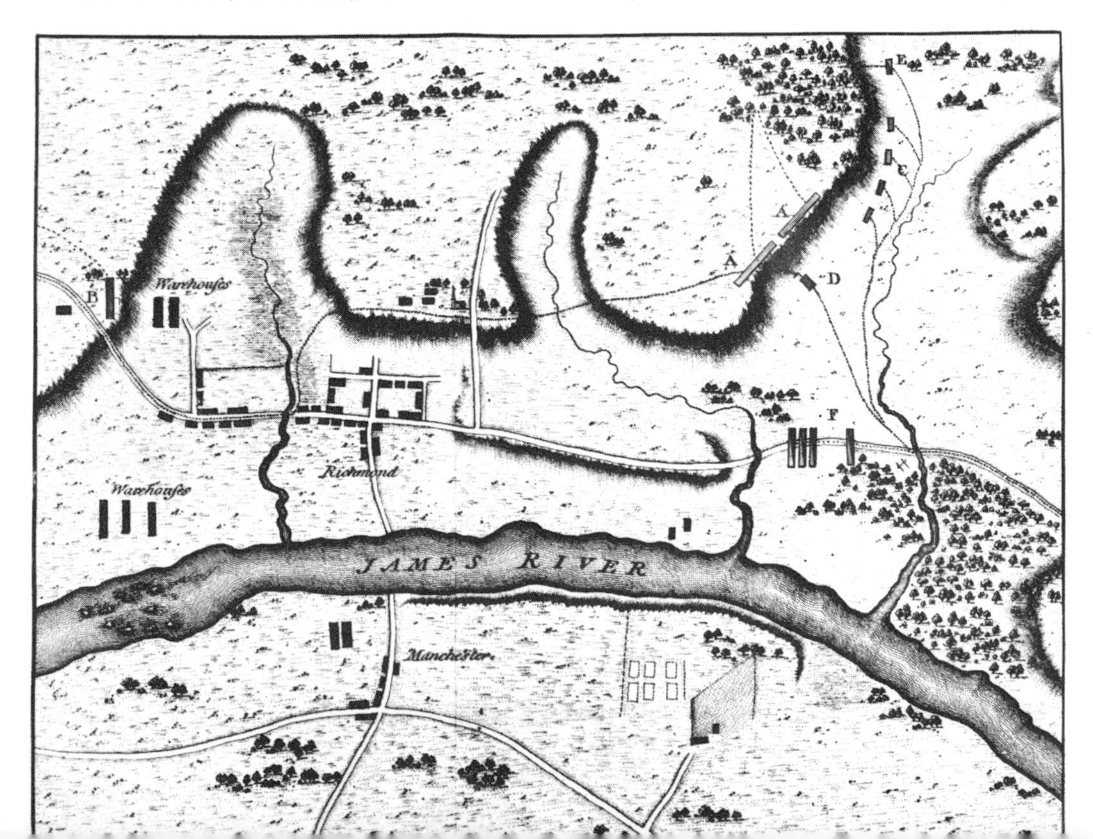

French troops march into the siege lines around Yorktown. On October 19, 1781

Many men thought only a dictatorship could save Virginia. Patrick Henry pressed the idea. Richard Henry Lee was recommending George Washington for the post. Jefferson's friends in the House of Delegates barely managed to frustrate the dictatorship movement, but Jefferson's own re-election was a practical impossibility.

Meeting June 12, the House of Delegates compromised by making Thomas Nelson, Jr., governor. He already commanded the militia.

But between electing Nelson and voting a pair of pistols and a sword to the dashing Jack Jouett, the House of Delegates did an astonishing and shocking thing. A young man named George Nicholas was making his first appearance as a delegate. He was pro-dictatorship. At Patrick Henry's instigation, or so Jefferson always suspected, Nicholas moved an investigation of Jefferson's conduct as governor.

Jefferson was not a delegate and could not speak for himself. His

Cornwallis surrendered his redcoats to Washington, and the Revolution was won.

friends could not oppose an investigation because it would look as though they feared the truth. So the House of Delegates voted to investigate Thomas Jefferson.

Jefferson did not know why he was being investigated and so he wrote to George Nicholas and asked why. Nicholas replied vaguely and rather apologetically. To the questions which Nicholas did ask about his administration, Jefferson gave frank and specific answers as he had always done during his career.

Before the investigating committee reported to the House on December 12, the French Admiral de Grasse had blockaded Chesapeake Bay, Washington and the French General Rochambeau had trapped Cornwallis at Yorktown, and the British had surrendered.

When it did act on the report, the House of Delegates voted Jefferson its "sincere thanks . . . for his impartial, upright, and attentive administration" and praised his "ability, rectitude, and integrity."

A PHILOSOPHER AT HOME
(1781-1784)

Nobody but Thomas Jefferson ever would have thought of putting a compass on the ceiling of the parlor.

"The Governor possesses a Noble Spirit of Building," a German officer prisoner, who was teaching himself English in Jefferson's "copious & well chosen Library," wrote home. "He is now finishing an elegant building, projected according to his own fancy. In his parlor he is creating on the Ceiling a Compass of his own invention by wich he can know the Strength as well as Direction of the Winds. I have promised to paint the Compass for it." The idea must have fascinated the Hamburg editor who published the letter in his newspaper.

Jefferson's compass and indicator, on the ceiling at Monticello, is connected to a weather vane located on the roof.

Jefferson's ceiling compass was but one of Monticello's many projected marvels. Now that the fight-

In Monticello's entrance hall is Jefferson's clock, operated by cannon-ball weights, which indicate the days of the week as they descend. The two pairs of antlers were brought back from Lewis and Clark's western expedition in 1806.

In Monticello's kitchen, Mrs. Jefferson read recipes aloud to Ursula, her cook.

ing had stopped, Jefferson hoped to get on with finishing the house.

From the beginning, the house had been destined to be different from anything in the country. Other men built in valleys. Jefferson picked a mountaintop. Other men built of wood. Jefferson built of brick. Other men, planning a house, called in a carpenter and told him vaguely what to do. Jefferson knew exactly what he wanted.

A skilled draftsman—Jefferson had learned the trade from his surveyor father—he drew designs, pondered them, set them aside, and started over. Jefferson disliked the clutter of outbuildings that spoiled many Virginia plantation houses and so he lodged his outbuildings—the kitchen, the laundry, the storerooms, the icehouse, the servants' rooms—underground. Connected to the house and concealed by walks and terraces, they were sheltered from rain, snow, wind, and blazing sun.

Long before the house was built, he had a plan for the grounds:

"Keep it in deer, rabbits, peacocks, guinea, poultry, pigeons, etc. Let it be an asylum for hares, squirrels, pheasants, partridges, and every other wild animal (except those of prey). Court them to it, by laying food for them in proper places. Procure a buck-elk, to be, as it were, monarch of the wood; but keep him shy, that his appearance may not lose its effect by too much familiarity. A buffalo might be confined also."

He provided for a fish pond, to keep captured trout alive until dinnertime. He planted an orchard of peaches, apples, cherries, apricots, pomegranates, figs, nectarines, quinces, walnuts, and almonds, as well as Mazzei's sour oranges and olives. He grafted trees and collected shrubs and experimented constantly with seeds of all kinds.

Jefferson eventually filled Monticello with ingenious gadgets. A clock in the entrance hall told not only the time, but by means of weights like cannon balls, the day of the week. A pair of doors, carefully synchronized with hidden ropes and pulleys, swung open together when a hand touched one. A dumb-waiter brought wine from the cellar. A revolving door with shelves expedited service between pantry and dining room and sheltered the diners from noise and heat. The drawing room boasted the first parquet floor (a floor of inlaid wood, arranged in patterns) in America.

Jefferson designed everything, including the furniture, the curtains, and a coffee urn. He not only designed, he fashioned. "He was," an old servant said, "as neat a hand as ever you saw to make keys and locks and small chains, iron and brass."

Visiting Jefferson, a French officer, the Marquis de Chastellux, wrote home: "We may safely aver, that Mr. Jefferson is the first American who has consulted the fine arts to know how he should shelter himself from the weather."

When the secretary of the French legation in Philadelphia, the Marquis François de Barbé-Marbois, began collecting data about America for his government, James Monroe's congressman uncle, Joseph Jones, referred him to Jefferson.

Resting at Poplar Forest after a fall from Caractacus, his horse, and his escape from Tarleton, Jefferson began preparing answers for the Marquis out of the vast store of information he had collected in the *Commonplace Books*, the *Account Books*, the *Farm Books*, the *Garden Book*. The eventual result was part almanac, part encyclopedia.

Do you have to know how far up the Nansemond River is navigable for 250-ton vessels? How long it takes to go by bateau from the Ohio's mouth to the Mississippi's? Where the Monacan Indians lived? How many guns a British ship of the line carried? How high the Natural Bridge—which Jefferson owned—rises above the river bed? The answers—and an incredible amount of other facts, figures, and fancies—are jammed into Jefferson's reply to the Marquis, or into the book which they eventually became. It was published as *Notes on the State of Virginia.*

In *Notes on the State of Virginia* Jefferson politely but firmly demolished the idea of the French Count de Buffon, greatest naturalist of the day, that animals were smaller in America than in Europe.

First, he relied on statistics. Later, when he was in France, he wrote to General John Sullivan of New Hampshire for the skin and skeleton of a moose to show to Buffon. Sullivan organized an expedition, killed the biggest moose he could find, cut a road through twenty-four miles of deep snow to get the moose out, added the horns of five other great deer to those of the moose, and shipped everything to France in a huge crate. The charges came to $150, dismaying Jefferson; but he may have felt the money well spent when

Mrs. William Thornton dated her watercolor of Monticello "1804," and said the house was in "unfinished state, 'tho commenced 27 years ago." Her dates are wrong, as Monticello was begun in 1768.

Buffon apologized: "I should have consulted you, Mr. Jefferson, before I wrote my *Natural History*."

Even before anyone had seen the book, Jefferson was elected to the American Philosophical Society along with George Washington and other distinguished citizens.

Then personal tragedy struck again, this time more cruelly than ever. Jefferson's entry in his *Account Book* for September 6, 1782, reads: "My dear wife died this day at 11:45 A.M." She had borne six children in ten years, the most recent a few months before. Three had died. She was 34 years old and her strength was gone. For four months Jefferson had rarely left her bedside.

Jefferson was not beside her when she died. He had been led from the room in a daze, and fainted in the library. His coma lingered until his sister Martha Carr feared he would never come to. Reviving, he shut the library door and walked to-and-fro the night through. Between naps forced on him by exhaustion, he strode the library floor for three weeks. Patsy watched over him. When he left the room, he mounted a horse to wander lonely trails.

In Philadelphia, Jefferson's friends were worried about him. If only they could get him back into public life. . . Someone suggested he be sent to Europe to help negotiate the peace with Britain, a task he previously had had to reject. He accepted. The two younger children went to their aunt, Mrs. Francis Eppes. He put Patsy in school in Philadelphia.

Jefferson prepared to sail from Baltimore on a French frigate, *Romulus*. But the *Romulus* was stuck in the ice. Once, toward the end of January, 1783, Jefferson heard the ship might break free. He hurried from Philadelphia toward Baltimore. It was a miserable five-day journey. He tried to get out to the *Romulus* to talk to its captain and the ice trapped his small boat. Meanwhile, seven British warships waited off the capes for the *Romulus* and Jefferson. He could not sail. The other commissioners negotiated the peace treaty, which was signed in Paris on September 3, 1783.

In Richmond, the House of Delegates was pleased at the opportunity to regain Jefferson's services for Virginia, and elected him to Congress. The prestige of Congress had never been lower, and when Jefferson set out to join it, it had fled from Philadelphia to Princeton to escape the protests of the unpaid troops. When Jefferson got to Princeton, it had moved again. He finally caught up with his colleagues in Annapolis in December.

In this brief period of congressional service, Jefferson did more to

Jefferson said that Natural Bridge—the 215-foot-high arch over Cedar Creek, on his property, near Lexington, Virginia—was the most sublime of nature's works.

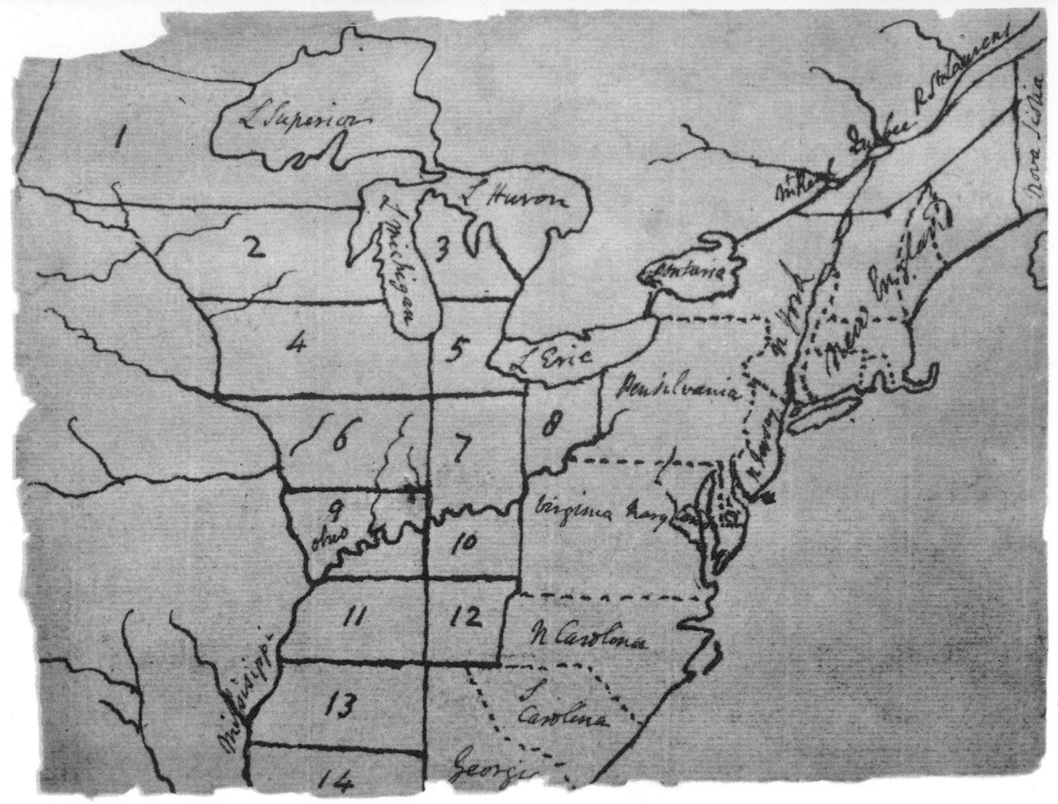

This map of fourteen new states proposed by Jefferson was drawn in 1784. As a member of the Continental Congress, he wanted slavery forbidden in the Northwest Territory. Congress refused his plan, but three years later (when Jefferson was in France) the Ordinance of 1787, or Northwest Ordinance, was passed. It stated that no man born in the Northwest Territory should be a slave.

shape the United States than most lawmakers can hope to achieve in a lifetime. One accomplishment dated back to his first trip to New York, another to an idea which he had put forward before the Revolution.

The Declaration of Independence had still been unwritten when Jefferson proposed that Virginia give up her western vastnesses. Under their own governments, he reasoned, they would develop faster.

In March, 1784, the Virginia delegation led by Jefferson handed Congress a deed to Virginia's lands northwest of the Ohio. Jefferson personally wanted Virginia to let Kentucky become a separate state.

But his ideas went far beyond mere cession of land by Virginia alone. He drew a map setting the boundaries of fourteen new states, some of them south of the Ohio. He even named the new states. Some of the names—Cherronesus, Assenisipia, and Pelisipia—were too complicated; others—Michigania and Illinoia—were more adaptable. More important than what he called them, he closed the new states to slavery after 1800.

Congress did not accept his plan, but it erected the famous Ordinance of 1787 on his foundations.

The other problem Jefferson tackled in this Congress was money.

It was still circulating in the confusion and variety he had encountered on his way to New York a generation back. Robert Morris proposed money based on the decimal system and Jefferson argued in his support: "Everyone remembers that, when learning Money-Arithmetic, he used to be puzzled with adding the farthings, taking out the fours and carrying them on; adding the pence, taking out the twelves and carrying them on; adding the shillings, take out the twenties and carrying them on, but when he came to the pounds, where he had only tens to carry forward, it was easy and free from error."

In a learned but still fascinating essay called "Notes on the Establishment of a Money Unit and of a Coinage for the United States," he told exactly how to keep the monetary system simple, and proposed the now familiar dollars, dimes, and pennies. Congress took his advice.

One wonders if Patsy did. She was still in Philadelphia and Jefferson was worried about her education. "The chance that in marriage she will draw a blockhead," he wrote to Marbois, "I calculate at about fourteen to one." And if she married a blockhead, the whole burden of educating her family would fall on her. So, four days after he arrived in Annapolis, he wrote Patsy an affectionate letter which told her how to spend her time:

> "From eight to ten, practice music.
> From ten to one, dance one day and draw another.
> From one to two, draw on the day you dance, and write a letter next day.
> From three to four, read French.
> From four to five, exercise yourself in music.
> From five till bed-time, read English, write and so forth."

But for both Patsy and Jefferson an exciting new life lay just ahead. In May, 1784, Congress appointed Jefferson a Minister Plenipotentiary, to join Benjamin Franklin and John Adams in negotiating treaties of commerce with European countries. Patsy and Jefferson sailed for Europe from Boston at 4 A.M. July 5, 1784, in the ship *Ceres*.

It would be quite a while before Jefferson could delight once more in the compass on the parlor ceiling.

In 1782, Jefferson entered his 34-year-old wife's death in his Account Book.

Sep. 5. lent Dr. Gilmer 5 lb sugar.
6. my dear wife died this day at 11H-45' A.M.
rec. by Richd. Gaines for tobo. [illegible] £29.
lent him 12/6

OUR MINISTER TO FRANCE

(1784-1789)

Hearing that Benjamin Franklin, America's representative in Paris, was going home for good, the Count de Vergennes, France's minister of foreign affairs, asked Jefferson: "You replace Monsieur Franklin?" Said Jefferson: "No one can replace him, sir: I am only his successor."

When Jefferson arrived in France he renewed his friendship with the Marquis de Lafayette, who had fought with the colonists in the Revolution. Because of Lafayette's friendship, every door in France opened to him; the wittiest women, the wisest statesmen and scientists competed to win him to their salons.

For most of Jefferson's first year abroad, Franklin was America's ranking representative in France. Congress wanted Jefferson and John Adams to help him negotiate commercial treaties, including an international guarantee under which unarmed merchant ships would be exempt from capture by nations which were at war.

Such a pact would endanger Britain's control of the sea. Britain would have none of it. When Jefferson and Adams went to London to seek a treaty of commerce, King

The gardens and Palace of Versailles.

George turned his back on them, and a general warned Jefferson that if the colonies wanted to rejoin the Empire, Britain would refuse them.

Other powers were more polite, but no more interested in the treaty: Only King Frederick of Prussia signed, and he had no navy.

In North Africa, the rulers of Morocco, Algiers, Tripoli, and Tunis

Here lived King Louis XVI of France, while many of his people were starving.

made King George seem courtly. Long before the word *racketeer* had been coined, these four Arab states had developed a brutal but profitable racket: they looted ships and enslaved the sailors of nations that did not pay richly to be let alone.

When the piratical powers seized three American ships, Jefferson became very angry. He was all for resistance. If we were going to be a maritime power, he wrote to James Monroe, who was now a congressman, this was the time to begin. Franklin and Adams calmed him, and Congress, aware of America's weaknesses, preferred to negotiate.

Then, in the spring of 1785, Franklin went home and Adams went to England as minister. By the time Jefferson succeeded Franklin as minister to France, and paid his respects to Louis XVI on May 14, he was a more experienced diplomat.

Jefferson spent his six weeks in England seeing what he could in factories and gardens. In a new steam-run grist mill, he extracted all there was to know about its equipment and fuel consumption. "A peck and a half of coal," he wrote to Charles Thomson, secretary of Congress, would do "exactly as much as a horse" could in a day. Applied to boats, he suggested, steam would "lay open all the streams to navigation," and he rejoiced that America had abundant coal.

Visiting Kew, he saw an Archimedes screw pump water. Draftsman Jefferson quickly made a sketch to send to America. He bought, besides books, a thermometer, a protractor, a globe telescope, a solar microscope, a hydrometer, a camp theodolite, and a harpsichord to be custom-built to his specifications.

Jefferson succeeded Benjamin Franklin as American Minister to France in 1785.

Wherever he was in Europe, he considered himself purchasing agent for friends in America. He sent Madison almost 200 books which influenced Madison's work on the new American Constitution. He bought the *Encyclopédie Méthodique* for American colleges, and for friends who would appreciate it.

He informed the presidents of Harvard, Yale, William and Mary, and the College of Philadelphia, and members of the American Philosophical Society, of such developments as an attempt to steer a manned balloon, and an experiment in running a ship by a steam-driven screw propeller.

Besides facts, he shipped living things—hares, rabbits, pheasants, partridges, wine grapes, cork trees—to enrich America.

Virginia had asked him to find an architect to design a state capitol. Jefferson long had dreamed secretly of a splendid group of government buildings which would give Richmond the dignity of a Rome or the grace of an Athens. He found an architect, but the capitol's design, based on a Roman temple at Nîmes, in France, was mostly Jefferson's. Virginia had asked him also

The ship that carried Polly Jefferson to Europe was met by Abigail Adams (above).

Jefferson visited our envoy to England, John Adams (above) in London, in 1786.

to find a sculptor to create a statue of Washington. Jefferson got Jean-Antoine Houdon to go to America. Houdon's *Washington* stands in the capitol at Richmond.

Jefferson, recovering from a broken wrist which did not set properly, toured southern France and northern Italy, cramming 21,000 useful words into his notebooks, and many more into his letters. At Nîmes, he saw for the first time the ancient building, the Maison Carrée, which had inspired his design for Virginia's capitol.

He investigated bridges, boats, canal locks. He went out of his way to find a Brazilian and discuss the possibility of Latin American revotion against Spain and Portugal. He studied the wine business and recommended against planting wine grapes where anything else would grow: too uncertain a crop. He marveled at olives: They would support a whole village, he said, on soil where corn would not feed a single family. He urged they be cultivated in America, and he shipped several dozen plants home.

He asked everyone why Carolina rice, which cost less and looked bet-

In Paris, Jefferson lived in the house shown at left: the Hôtel de Langeac.

Jefferson's daughter, Martha ("Patsy") was with him in France.

Jefferson met beautiful Maria Cosway in Paris in August, 1786.

Jefferson visited the Halle aux Blés (below) in Paris in 1786, particularly to see its "noble dome." It was: ". . . wonderful . . . the most superb thing on earth."

Jefferson hoped to have a similar dome built over a market in Richmond; the building also influenced his design for the University of Virginia's Rotunda.

King Louis XVI ruled France during Jefferson's stay in Paris.

Extravagant Queen Marie Antoinette was hated by the French.

ter, did not outsell rice from Lombardy. Replies conflicted, so he set out across the Alps, astride hired mules when a carriage could not make the grades. In Italy, he found export of seed rice forbidden under penalty of death. So he hired a muleteer named Poggio to smuggle a sackful to Genoa. Poggio never arrived but Jefferson had stuffed his own overcoat pockets with seed rice, which he sent to the Carolinas.

Through friends—including a prince of Cochin China—he acquired samples of other varieties from all over the world. But most of them grew in water and the people who worked them often died of malaria. So Jefferson turned to finding a dry rice and eventually tracked down a kind that thrived on Africa's mountains. In all, his researches helped to make Carolina rice some of the best in the world.

Jefferson and Patsy wanted to see Polly and Lucy Elizabeth who had remained in America. Jefferson planned to bring them to Europe but had made no definite arrangements for a voyage when Mr. and Mrs. Eppes sadly wrote that Lucy Elizabeth and one of their own daughters had died.

Polly's trip was not easily arranged. To reduce risk, Jefferson ruled she might travel only between March's end and August's beginning, in a proven ship less than five years old, belonging to a country that paid off the African pirates.

To complicate things, Polly did not want to leave America, and she scrawled a note to Dear Papa: ". . . I hope that you will send me a doll. I am very sorry that you have sent for me. I don't want to go to France, I had rather stay with Aunt Eppes. Your most happy and dutiful daughter, Polly Jefferson."

It took a trick to get her on her way. Every day she and her cousins were sent to play aboard ship. They soon felt quite at home, and the day the vessel was to sail, they were all sent below decks to nap. As Polly slumbered, her cousins were whisked ashore. Polly did not wake until she was at sea. Her tears once dry, she fell in love with the ship's captain, and did not want to leave the vessel when it reached England.

But Polly eventually reached Paris—after having become very fond of passengers on the coach—and once she got to know her father and her sister she loved them, too.

Soon after arriving in France, Jefferson had written home: "It is difficult to conceive how so good a people, with so good a king, ... so genial a climate, so fertile a soil, should be rendered so ineffectual for producing human happiness by . . . . a bad form of government." He added that "Of twenty millions of people . . . in France . . . there are nineteen millions more wretched . . . than the most conspicuously wretched individual of the whole of the United States." Perhaps Jefferson

On October 5, 1789, a Parisian mob took the King and Queen of France prisoners at Versailles and forced them to return with them to live in Paris.

exaggerated, but reform was indeed urgent. Mismanagement, corruption, and the extravagances and wars of Louis XIV and Louis XV had brought France to the brink of national bankruptcy.

When Jefferson began his trip south at the end of February, 1787, a Council of Notables, called by the well-meaning King Louis XVI, was chattering vehemently at Versailles about what to do.

Across the Atlantic, another council, the Constitutional Convention, was gathering in Philadelphia.

The American Revolution had become a Paris fashion: every American in France had become a model of the free man. Lafayette and his young officers had imported from America the very latest in ideas and, significantly, Lafayette was a member of the Council of Notables.

At this moment, in this atmosphere, peaceable reform was within France's reach: The King and his more liberal advisers made striking concessions which, Jefferson wrote, "came from the very heart of the King," who "had no wish but for the good of the nation."

Lafayette admired Jefferson's judgment in the affairs of government. In order to get his advice for France, Lafayette involved Jefferson beyond the bounds of diplomatic propriety. The Marquis brought seven "leading Patriots, of honest but different opinions," to Jefferson's house for dinner one day and from four in the afternoon to ten in the evening, over Jefferson's wine, they argued on what to do about the King and his reform offers.

The advice Jefferson gave to America and to France seems, at first, strikingly contradictory. Hearing of Shays' Rebellion in Massachusetts, which was an uprising of small farmers and debtors over taxes which they felt were ruining them and helping the powerful merchants, he wrote:

"God forbid we should ever be 20 years without such a rebellion . . . What country can preserve its liberties if its rulers are not warned from time to time that their people preserve the spirit of resistance? Let them take arms . . . The tree of liberty must be refreshed from time to time with the blood of patriots & tyrants. It is its natural manure."

But on the French he pressed moderation. Keep your king, advised the hater of kings. Follow the good model of England, he told Lafayette, by going "step by step towards a good Constitution . . . if every advance is to be purchased by filling the royal coffers with gold, it will be gold well employed."

The French winter of 1788–1789 was a dreadful one. Jefferson recorded temperatures of 18 below zero, Fahrenheit. Outdoor work was impossible and, lacking work, the poor lacked food and fuel. The government had to keep great bonfires blazing at Paris street corners to save people from freezing to death. Bread was so scarce, even for those who could pay, that "in cards of invitation to dine in the richest houses," Jefferson wrote, "the guest was notified to bring his own bread."

In these dangerous times the Marquis de Lafayette drew up a Declaration of the Rights of Man—modeled on Jeffersonian ideas—and the new National Assembly began writing a Constitution embracing it. Louis, influenced by conservative ministers and by his equally conservative Queen, Marie-Antoinette, confronted the people with troops instead of reforms, and Jefferson witnessed the beginning of real trouble.

Jefferson saw the first popular uprisings in Paris which led to the storming of the Bastille, symbol of the government's power. The Bastille was a fortress-prison in Paris where political prisoners were kept. He wrote descriptions of the attack on the Bastille by the revolutionaries led by his friend, Monsieur de Corny, and he also wrote a description of the surrender of the prison.

"They took all the arms, discharged the prisoners, and such of the garrison as were not killed in the

Lafayette was made commander of the National Guard, to keep order in Paris.

The real outbreak of the French Revolution took place on July 14, 1789, when an angry Parisian mob stormed the King's hated fortress-prison, the Bastille.

Here the Governor—Marquis de Launay—and his troops surrender to the crowd. Soon after, his head was chopped off, and prisoners in the Bastille were freed.

first moment of fury; carried the Governor and Lieutenant Governor to the Place de Grève (the place of public execution), cut off their heads, and sent them through the city, in triumph, to the Palais royal."

The king went to bed, Jefferson remarked, "fearfully impressed" and "had he been left to himself, he would have willingly acquiesced" in whatever the people's representatives decided was best for France.

Across the ocean between him and the Constitutional Convention in Philadelphia, Jefferson corresponded steadily with Madison, Monroe, Washington, and other friends, telling them how he stood.

In November, Jefferson got a copy of the Constitution that the Constitutional Convention had drafted. Most of it he approved. But he was disturbed by the absence of a Bill of Rights and of a specific ban on a life term for the President.

Jefferson again took the moderate course. Accept the Constitution as it is, he counseled—the suggestion actually was made first by Massachusetts—and improve it as soon as you can.

The Bill of Rights, proposed to Congress by Madison, was in process of ratification by the states when Jefferson started from Paris for Le Havre with Patsy and Polly on September 26, 1789. He had finally obtained permission to take a vacation, and they were homeward bound. They were still in Le Havre, waiting for a tempest to abate, when King Louis and Marie-Antoinette were taken prisoners by the leaders of the French revolutionaries.

Patsy Jefferson recorded the information that the *Clermont*, the ship taking the Jeffersons home, ran into rough weathering off Virginia and caught fire, after the passengers had disembarked, in Norfolk.

Norfolk gave Jefferson an official welcome and soon he received the surprising information that President Washington—who had been inaugurated April 30—had chosen him to be Secretary of State. It was an honor he did not really want as he wished to return to his post in France. Return to the peace and quiet of Monticello and his family was the most important thing for the moment, however.

Patsy described the homecoming:

"We reached Monticello on the 23rd of December. The Negroes . . . collected in crowds around it and almost drew it up the mountain by hand. The shouting, etc. . . had been sufficiently obstreperous before, but the moment it arrived at the top, it reached the climax. Then the door of the carriage was opened, they received him in their arms and bore him to the house, crowding around and kissing his hands and feet—some blubbering and crying—others laughing. It seemed impossible to satisfy their anxiety to touch and kiss the very earth which bore him."

THE GENIUS OF THOMAS JEFFERSON

"He who receives an idea from me, receives instruction himself without lessening mine; as he who lights his taper at mine receives light without darkening me." —T. J.

JEFFERSON
THE ARCHITECT

". . . how is a taste in this beautiful art to be formed in our countrymen unless we avail ourself of every occasion when public buildings are to be erected, of presenting to them models for their study and imitation?" —T. J.

Thomas Jefferson was sixty years old in 1803 when the prominent American artist Rembrandt Peale painted this portrait.

This drawing of the front of Poplar Forest, the house that Jefferson built near Lynchburg as a retreat from the busy life of Monticello, was made by one of his grandchildren, Cornelia Randolph.

Jefferson submitted this design for a national capitol to the government; he signed it "A.Z." to keep his name secret. He had been impressed with the domes designed by the 16th century Italian architect Palladio and used one in this design.

Jefferson called the Maison Carrée at Nîmes, France " . . . the most beautiful and precious morsel of architecture left to us by the ancients." His designs for the Virginia capitol and many other buildings were based on this Roman temple. ►

The building of the central section of Brandon, in Prince George County, Virginia, was influenced by a love for classic architecture which Jefferson brought back from Europe.

Jefferson designed the Virginia state capitol in Richmond when he was American Minister in France. He had a plaster model made of his design. This may be the original model.

JEFFERSON

THE INVENTOR

"Determine never to be idle. No person will have occasion to complain of the want of time who never loses any. It is wonderful how much may be done if we are always doing." —T. J.

Jean Houdon, the great French sculptor, made this bust of Jefferson in Paris in 1789—when Jefferson was forty-six.

When traveling by carriage, Jefferson used the odometer (above, right) to measure the number of miles he had covered. Because he had so many official and personal letters to write, Jefferson had the ingenious polygraph machine (below) built so that each letter he composed was copied while he was actually writing.

The dumbwaiter (above) was concealed in a fireplace at Monticello and was used to bring wine up from the cellar. The quartet stand (below), designed by Jefferson, who was an amateur violinist, was made at Monticello and could hold the sheet music of four musicians.

Jefferson's swivel chair (above) proved to be practical and its design is still copied today. Jefferson's political enemies called it his "whirligig chair."

JEFFERSON
THE NATURAL HISTORIAN

Jefferson is seen here as he appeared at forty-four, in 1787. Jefferson sat for the artist, John Trumbull, in Paris.

Thomas Jefferson was head of the American Philosophical Society when that organization financed the excavation of the bones of a prehistoric mastodon that had been found on a farm in Ulster County, New York. The excavation was directed by Charles Willson Peale, the prominent American artist, in 1801. Peale was an old friend of Thomas Jefferson. Peale first hired an expert wheelwright named Campbell to construct a giant pumping system to get rid of the water that kept filling the excavation. The system can be seen in this painting which Peale made of the operation, called Exhuming the First American Mastodon. *He later exhibited the bones and the painting in Philadelphia. Jefferson had long been interested in American animal life and had been called "Mr. Mammoth" by his political enemies because of his own collection of prehistoric bones. He often added to Peale's collection of fossil bones with his most prized specimens.*

"The passage of the Potomac through the Blue Ridge is perhaps one of the most stupendous scenes in nature. . . . It hurries our senses into the opinion that the mountains were formed first; that the rivers began to flow afterwards; in this place dammed up by the Blue Ridge Mountains . . ."

—T. J.

The American moose, seen in this drawing by James Audubon, was used by Jefferson in winning an argument with the famous French natural historian, Count Georges de Buffon. Jefferson sent the skin, horns, and skeleton of a huge moose—shot in New Hampshire—to France so that Buffon might see that he was wrong in saying that the animals of America were smaller than those of Europe.

JEFFERSON

THE SCIENTIST

". . . the acquisition of science is a pleasing employment . . The possession of it . . . will . . . render you dear to your friends, and give you fame and promotion in your own country." —T. J.

Jefferson is seen at seventy-eight, five years before his death, in this portrait done by the artist Thomas Sully in 1821.

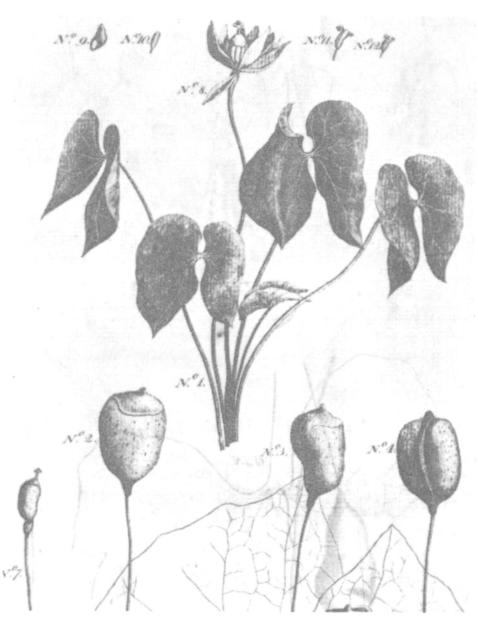

Jeffersonia diphylla, *the herb pictured above, was named in honor of Jefferson's contribution to the science of botany in America. At Monticello, Jefferson kept a record of his experiments with plants and with fruit trees in his Garden Books.*

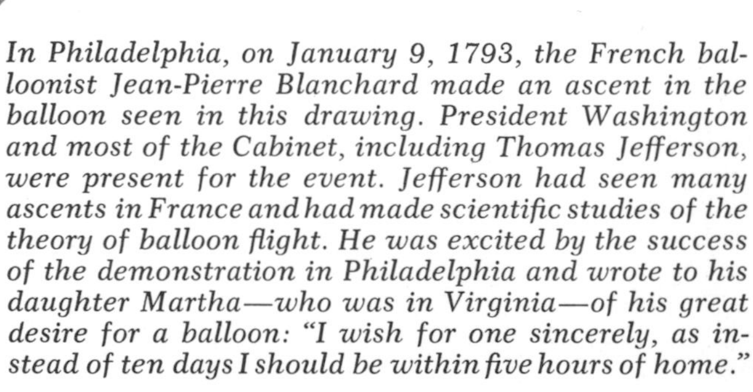

In Philadelphia, on January 9, 1793, the French balloonist Jean-Pierre Blanchard made an ascent in the balloon seen in this drawing. President Washington and most of the Cabinet, including Thomas Jefferson, were present for the event. Jefferson had seen many ascents in France and had made scientific studies of the theory of balloon flight. He was excited by the success of the demonstration in Philadelphia and wrote to his daughter Martha—who was in Virginia—of his great desire for a balloon: "I wish for one sincerely, as instead of ten days I should be within five hours of home."

Eli Whitney's cotton gin, seen in operation in this drawing, was granted a patent by Jefferson. As Secretary of State, the new Patent Office was placed under his control. On November 16, 1793, he wrote an enthusiastic personal letter to Whitney, telling him that the patent would be granted and expressing his own interest in knowing further facts about the machine: "As . . . Virginia . . . carries on manufacture of cotton . . . as I do myself, and one of our great embarrassments is the clearing of the cotton of the seed . . . I feel considerable interest in the success of your invention."

)r. Joseph Priestly (below), an ;nglishman and one of the founlers of modern chemistry, spent en years in America. He often xchanged letters with Jefferson.

This telescope of Jefferson's is the one he used at Monticello to observe the positions of comets, stars, and planets.

JEFFERSON
THE AGRARIAN

". . . Those who labour in the earth are the chosen people of God . . . whose breasts he has made his peculiar deposit for . . . genuine virtue."
—T. J.

This portrait of Jefferson by Rembrandt Peale was painted in 1800. Although it is one of the most famous likenesses because of the engravings made from it, the original was lost and not found until 1959.

Jefferson wanted his country to be a great farming nation. He imported trees and plants from all over the world to enrich the variety of things American farmers could grow. He brought apricots, wine grapes, and olives from Europe. He decided that America's native Carolina rice should be able to compete on the world market with rice from any part of the world and so he crossed Carolina rice with Italian rice—he had to have the seed smuggled out of Italy—with famous Chinese rice, and with dry, African rice. Jefferson's plan worked and America became a major world producer of rice.

Rice Birds and Rice

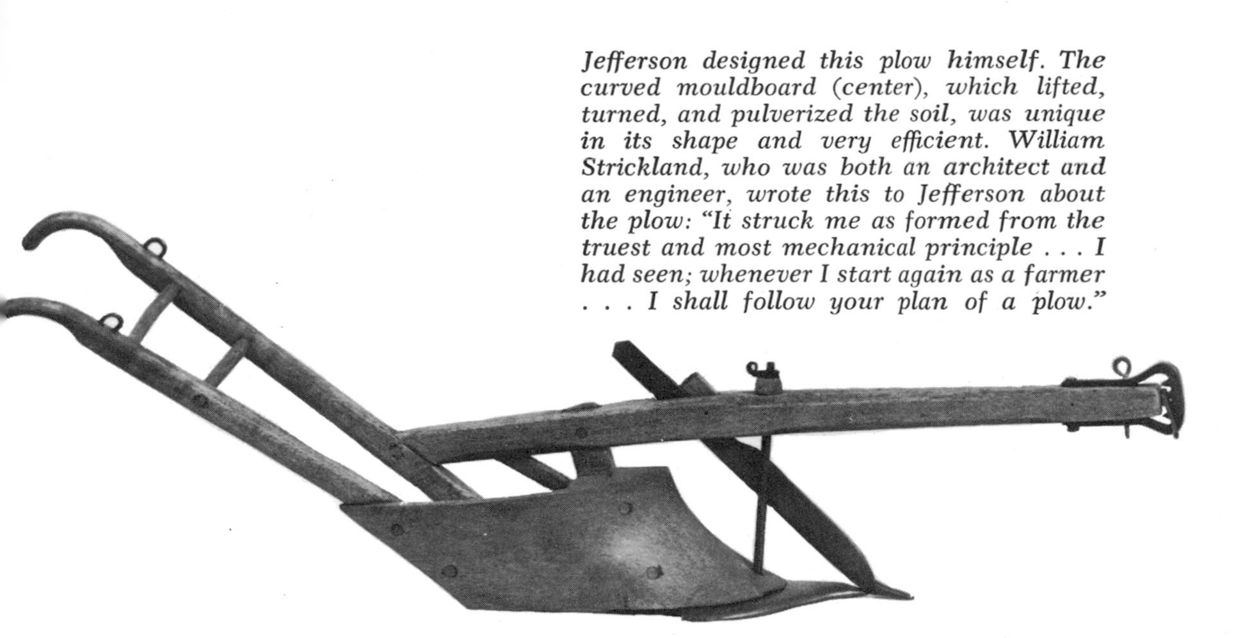

Jefferson designed this plow himself. The curved mouldboard (center), which lifted, turned, and pulverized the soil, was unique in its shape and very efficient. William Strickland, who was both an architect and an engineer, wrote this to Jefferson about the plow: "It struck me as formed from the truest and most mechanical principle . . . I had seen; whenever I start again as a farmer . . . I shall follow your plan of a plow."

Jefferson had been more impressed with the gardens he saw in England than with the houses they surrounded. This plan for a garden—taken from his Garden book—was intended for the grounds of Monticello and shows that he wanted to plant a great many fragrant shrubs—including lilacs, cape jasmine (gardenias), and Persian jasmine.

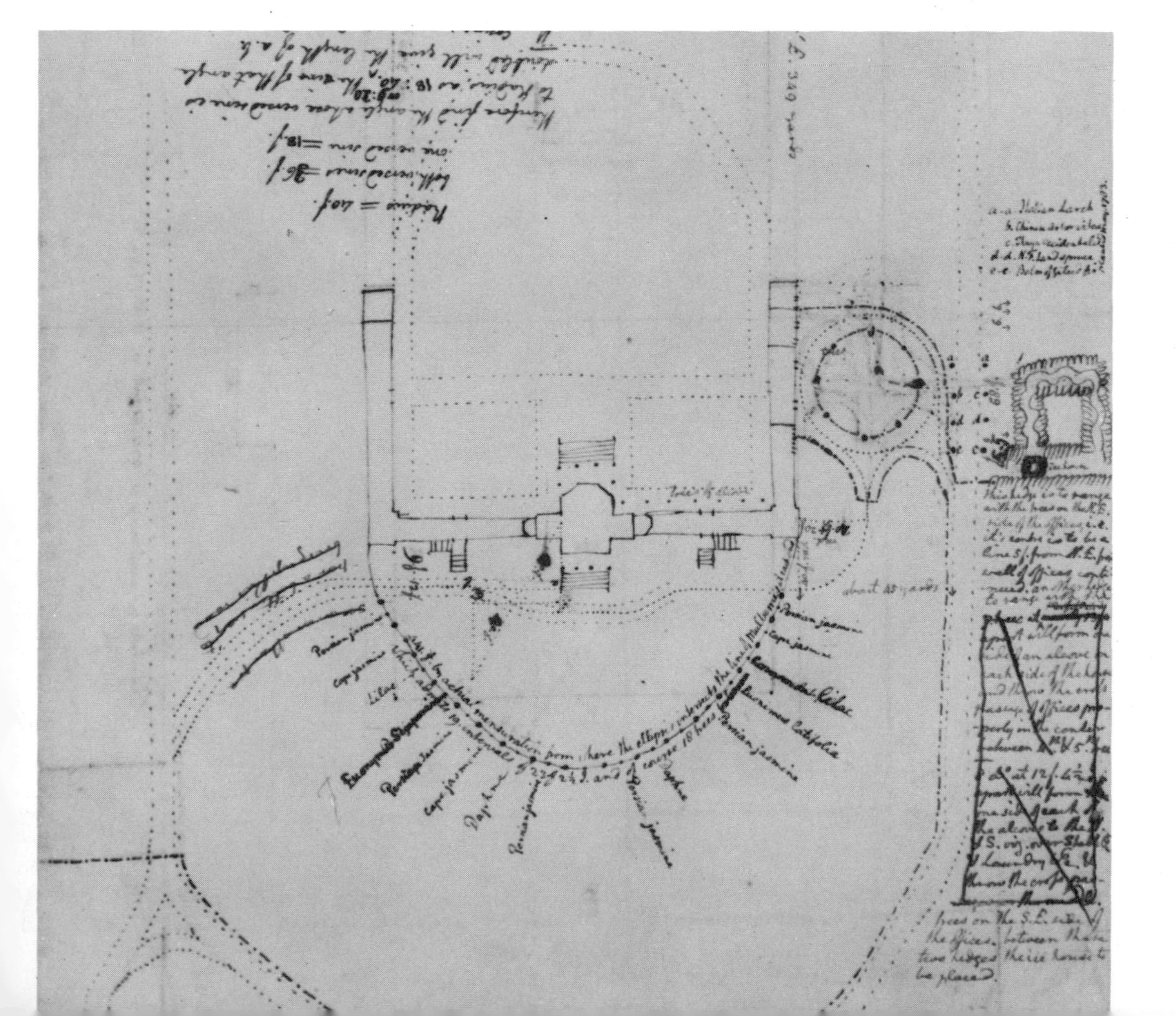

JEFFERSON

THE INTELLECTUAL

"... the flames kindled on the 4th of July, 1776, have spread over too much of the globe to be extinguished by the feeble engines of despotism; on the contrary, they will consume these engines and all who work them." —T. J.

This last likeness of Jefferson, a life mask, was made when he was eighty-two, in 1825. He died in the following year.

Jefferson had surrounded himself with books all his life. His ideas, contained in the Virginia Constitution and in the Declaration of Independence, were formed by the great writers of the 18th century enlightenment: Voltaire, Rousseau, Locke and many others. Jefferson's reading also influenced the Constitution, for he sent James Madison —most important in forming that document— a box of 200 books from Paris in which the French and English political thinkers were represented. His own great library, sold to raise money in his old age, forms the basis of the Library of Congress.

This painting shows the voting on the United States Constitution by the Constitutional Convention on September 17, 1787. Key figures in the making of the Constitution were George Washington (standing on platform at right), the elderly Benjamin Franklin (standing at left), James Madison (seated far left), and Alexander Hamilton (seated far right). Jefferson's duties in Paris as American Minister kept him from the meetings which shaped the document and finally adopted it. His friend James Madison, however, frequently consulted him by mail and got Jefferson's reactions to the work that was being done. Jefferson did not like the Constitution's lack of a bill of rights—such as Virginia had—and he did not like the amount of power it gave the federal government. When Madison wrote to tell him that the Constitution had been adopted and was to be ratified by the states, Jefferson still objected to the features he had found missing to begin with. Still, he encouraged Madison to work for its ratification because, he said: "It is a good canvas, on which some strokes only want retouching." It was in many ways a document much to the liking of the man who had written the Declaration of Independence.

This portrait of Jefferson was painted by Gilbert Stuart, the famous American artist, sometime between 1799 and 1800, when Jefferson was about fifty-seven.

JEFFERSON
THE HUMANITARIAN

". . . for I have sworn upon the altar of God, eternal hostility against every form of tyranny over the mind of man." —T. J.

This cartoon, in its attempt to make fun of the customs and dress of a religious group—in this case, the Quakers—is typical of the kind of thinking that Jefferson was fighting when he wrote Virginia's Act for Religious Freedom, which passed in 1786. This Act advanced the cause of religious freedom in the whole country.

Jefferson hated slavery all his life. He played an important role in stopping the slave trade in Virginia and in banning slavery in the Western states. This picture shows the beating of a Negro—the sort of cruelty that Jefferson found unpardonable.

Logan, the Mingo chief

Isaac Jefferson

The strong feelings which Thomas Jefferson had for the rights of the individual grew from his close knowledge of the people he wanted most to help. He had known and been interested in Indians all his life. When Logan, the Indian chief pictured above, told the story of the massacre of his family by white soldiers in colonial times, Jefferson recorded it in his Account Book as an example of the evil men do to one another. He was kind to slaves of his own and gave many of them their freedom upon his death. Isaac, his slave, pictured above in a daguerreotype from the 1840's, was the son of Monticello's pastry cook, Ursula, nicknamed Queenie; and of her husband who was called King George.

Jefferson was very interested in learning Indian languages. This is a page from his Indian vocabulary.

English	fog	rain	snow
French	brouillard	pluie	neige
Delaware	aawan	suuklan	uiina
[illegible]ami	....	su-ke-laan	guun
Monsi	....	su-ke-laan	guun
Chippewa	....	ke-me-wàn	ac-guun
Knisteneaux	pakisbihow	kimiwoin	counah
Algonquin	awinni	ki mi woini	so qui po
Tawa	....	ki-mi-wàn	ac-guùn
Shawanee	....	kè-mè-waini kimmawane	[illegible] loode
Nanticoke	[illegible]	uiniaw su-k[illegible]an	quo-no quun
Mohiccon	....	sokan[illegible]an so-ke[illegible]an	washaná wa-scha-ni
[illegible]nquachog	....	sùhenun	soáchpo
Oneida	[illegible]	yoconnoal	onaiephla
Cayuga	....	....	....
Onondaga	[illegible]	[illegible]	ogéra
Miami	.... [illegible]	petelénive petilanuah	monètwa monatush
Cherokee	....	[illegible]	[illegible]

SECRETARY OF STATE
(1790-1793)

Patsy did not marry a blockhead, as her father had feared.

A few months after the Jeffersons arrived home, she became the bride of Thomas Mann Randolph, her second cousin. Jefferson considered Randolph "a young gentleman of genius, science, and honorable mind."

Jefferson found himself in need of money after he returned home, despite the many acres of fertile land he owned. He had to write to Amsterdam, the money-lending center of Europe, to try to borrow one or two thousand dollars. His farms had not prospered during his absence. His salary in Paris had not covered his expenses.

But his burdensome debts—some 7,500 pounds sterling—resulted from his honesty, not his improvidence. When his father-in-law John Wayles died back in 1773, Jefferson sold some of the Wayles's land to pay the debts of the estate. The buyers gave Jefferson notes, or signed promises to pay. The estate's Scottish and English creditors refused to accept the buyers' notes, but willingly took Jefferson's.

When war came, Virginia forbade payments on the notes to the enemy and borrowed the money instead for its own needs. After the war it paid back the loans, but in nearly worthless paper currency. Under the circumstances, some Virginians considered their debts to Britons wiped out. Jefferson started paying all over again.

Jefferson really could not afford to accept the $3,500-a-year post as Secretary of State that Congressman Madison, visiting Monticello as President Washington's emissary, urged on him. He left Monticello on March 1, however, for the journey to New York, then the nation's capital. He could refuse Washington nothing.

Jefferson disliked the Federalists' courtly receptions—like this one of Lady Washington's—which took place in New York during George Washington's Presidency.

With 33,000 residents and a length of a mile and a half at its longest, New York was nothing like Paris. President Washington's Broadway mansion did not resemble the Palace of Versailles, nor did George Washington in any way think of himself as a king.

But the city's political climate disturbed Jefferson. Washington was surrounded by courtiers, and Jefferson quickly discovered that "a preference of kingly, over republican, government, was evidently the favorite sentiment." He was "feasted from table to table" and at every table "found myself . . . the only advocate on the republican side."

Jefferson's old friends John Adams and Richard Henry Lee had seriously argued that the President should have an impressive title and the Senate just as seriously had decided on "His Highness the President of the United States and Protector of Their Liberties."

Jefferson's friend, Madison, dryly sent the proposal back from the

House of Representatives with the comment that the President already had a title fixed by the Constitution: "The President of the United States." Adams already had a title too, but he did not know it. He was stout and people had nicknamed him "Rotundity."

Abigail Adams, John's plain, generally sensible wife, wrote approvingly to her sister that the President rode only in a six-horse coach, accompanied by four servants and two gentleman riders. The coach was cream-colored. Washington almost seemed to be taking the advice of Adams, who was Vice-President. Adams had said that without "splendor and majesty" neither "dignity nor authority" could be maintained, and that without "state and pomp" the United States would hope in vain for other nations' respect.

The nation's respectable people sided with Adams and among his fellow cabinet members, Jefferson found few allies of republicanism.

The Secretary of the Treasury was young Alexander Hamilton, as remarkable a man as Jefferson, but quite different. Orphaned and apprenticed in a store before he was thirteen, he dreamed of making a better life for himself. A hurricane blew him on his way. When it struck the West Indian island of St. Croix, where he lived, he penned so dramatic a description of it that local folk collected money to send him to the mainland to study. At seventeen, attending Columbia University, which was then called King's College, he wrote lively pamphlets pressing the colonial cause. At nineteen, he was General Washington's aide and a lieutenant colonel. At thirty-four, he was Secretary of the Treasury. He admired Britain's monarchy so much that he shocked Thomas Jefferson.

Jefferson could understand Adams, the old republican: he had been overwhelmed by the "glare of roy-

My dear Maria — New York June 13. 1790.

I have recieved your letter of May 23. which was in answer to mine of May 2. but I wrote you also on the 23d. of May, so that you still owe me an answer to that, which I hope is now on the road. in matters of correspondence as well as of money you must never be in debt. I am much pleased with the account you give me of your occupations, and the making the pudding is as good an article of them as any. when I come to Virginia I shall insist on eating a pudding of your own making, as well as on trying other specimens of your skill. you must make the most of your time while you are with so good an aunt who can learn you every thing. [illegible] peas nor strawberries here till the 8th. day of this month. on the same day I heard the first Whip-poor-will whistle. swallows and martins appeared here on the 21st. of April. when did they appear with you? and when had you peas, strawberries, & whip-poor-wills in Virginia? take notice hereafter whether the whip-poor-wills always come with the strawberries & peas. send me a copy of the maxims I gave you, also a list of the books I promised you. [illegible] had a long touch of my periodical head-ach, but a very moderate one. it has not quite left me yet. Adieu, my dear, love your uncle aunt & cousins, and me more than all.

Your's affectionately,

Th: Jefferson.

Miss Maria Jefferson.

This letter—one of 18,000 Jefferson wrote in his lifetime—went to his 12-year-old daughter, Mary, in Virginia.

alty and nobility" and frightened by Shays' Rebellion during his term as minister in England. But of Hamilton, "acute . . . disinterested, honest and honorable in all private transactions," he could say only that the young man had been "bewitched and perverted."

As Secretary of State, Jefferson had responsibilities bigger than his staff of five could handle. He had been in New York only a few weeks when Congress set up a Patent Office to protect inventors' rights to their inventions. Jefferson was assigned the job as part of his domestic responsibility as Secretary of State. His interest in science made him particularly well-suited to run the Patent Office, but the work made great demands on his time.

One of the Patent Office's first applicants for a patent was a man named Eli Whitney. Whitney invented a device for removing the seed from a boll of cotton called a cotton gin.

Congress asked Jefferson if he thought this country should mint its own coins or farm out the job to some European nation. His reply resulted in the establishment of the Philadelphia Mint, of which he was given supervision. He proposed a decimal system of weights and measures, which would have made schoolboys' lives a good deal happier had it been adopted. Ten inches would make a foot, ten feet a decad, ten decads a rood, ten roods a furlong and ten furlongs a mile. He wanted to standardize weights, as well.

Over two months later, Mary Jefferson (nicknamed "Maria" and "Polly") answered her "Dear Papa's" questions about peas, strawberries, and whippoorwills.

1790

Dear Papa

I have just received your
favour July 23 and am determined to
to you every day till I have discharged
debt. when we were in Cumberland we
Church and heard some singing Masters that
very well they are to come here to learn my
ins to sing and as I know you have no
tions to my learning any thing I am to
scholar and hope to give you the pleasu
earing an anthem we had pease the 10 of may
strawberries the 17 of the same month tho
in that abundance we are accustomed to in

Jefferson Maria. recd Aug.

consequence of a frost this spring as for the
martins swallows and whippoorwills I was so
taken up with my chickens that I never attend
ed to them and therefore cannot tell you when
they came tho I was so unfortunate as to lose half
of them for my cousin Bolling and myself have
raised but 18 between us adieu my Dear Papa
believe me to be your affectionate daughter
Mary Jefferson

Mr Jefferson New York

All these chores were extra duty: the Secretary of State's major concern, of course, was foreign policy. Seven years after the signing of the peace treaty in 1783, the British still held outposts on the northwest frontier. They gave the excuse that the United States had not yet carried out its obligations under the agreement in which Britain agreed to give up the outposts. For a time, the British refused to send an official diplomatic representative: they dealt with the United States diplomatically only through an unofficial agent, a man named Beckwith.

Spain not only held Florida, but dominated the Mississippi. Settlers in Kentucky and Tennessee could not send their goods to market without passing through Spanish customs at New Orleans.

France imposed fewer restrictions on our imports than did Britain, but most of our trade was with Britain, and Britain would not even admit into the West Indies imports brought in American ships.

Early in 1793 American Federalists heard with sorrow that France had guillotined King Louis XVI, and become a republic.

When the British and Spanish seemed about to fight over Britain's intrusion in what is now British Columbia, Jefferson shrewdly and coldly tried to play one against the other to gain advantages for America.

Tackling tariffs, Jefferson was equally realistic and equally unsuccessful. He believed in free trade, and thought that the ideal situation would be one in which every country produced "that which nature has best fitted it to produce" and sold it everywhere without restrictions. But the ideal was not possible yet, he realized. So he proposed instead a working policy of give-and-take. If France gives us favorable tariff rates, give France favorable rates. If Britain excluded our ships, exclude British ships.

Jefferson's varied burdens changed him not a bit. On June 13, 1790, he wrote to George Wythe, back home: . . . "I enclose a few seeds of highland rice which was gathered last autumn in the East Indies . . . I have sowed a few seeds in earthen pots . . ." The rice had been brought from the Moluccas to London by a Lieutenant Bligh, later the famous captain of the *Bounty*.

Jefferson went home to Monticello for a visit in August. When he returned to work in November, his job was now in Philadelphia, which had become the capital. He rented a house there which he furnished with the contents of 86 packing cases just arrived from France.

The taverns of Philadelphia were to have Congressional customers for only ten years. After that the capital would move to a new city on the Potomac. It was Jefferson who assigned Major Andrew Ellicott—assisted by a Negro mathematician named Benjamin Banneker—to survey the site.

After the government moved away from New York, and Philadelphia became the capital in the fall of 1790, George Washington lived here, on High Street.

It was Jefferson who instructed Major Pierre Charles L'Enfant, the French veteran of Washington's army who had been engaged to design the city. And it was Jefferson who fired L'Enfant when he proved arrogant and illegally tore down a house that stood in his way.

Another Frenchman was to cause Jefferson, the friend of France, a great deal more trouble.

The news that France had declared herself a republic in September, 1792, sparked exuberant rejoicing all over America. Boston celebrated with a parade and a giant barbecue. The enthusiasm cooled considerably when word arrived in mid-March that King Louis had been executed and that Marie-Antoinette was imprisoned and likely to be condemned to death. Furthermore France had declared war on February 1, 1793 on Britain, Spain, and Holland.

But republican France's new minister, a young man named Edmond Charles Genêt, got a lively popular welcome when he debarked at Charleston, South Carolina, from the frigate *Embuscade* on April 8, 1793. As Genêt headed north by land to Philadelphia, Washington and his Cabinet debated vigorously what to do with him.

France was an ally. The United States was committed by treaty to defend the French West Indies in case of attack. If the government received Genêt as minister, would it become involved in France's war?

Hamilton argued that the treaty had been made with the French king: When the French killed their king, the treaty ceased to exist.

Jefferson retorted that treaties were made with nations, not individuals, and were not affected when the head of state changed. The United States has pursued this policy ever since.

But nobody was eager to become involved in the war. Jefferson supported the decision to proclaim American neutrality. Genêt was received in Philadelphia with official coolness.

American neutrality puzzled, astonished, and infuriated Genêt. Was not this the land Frenchmen had helped to free? Had not Jefferson seen the welcome the *Embuscade* got when it arrived in Philadelphia from Charleston with a British ship captured on the way.

Jefferson explained to Genêt that the President had proclaimed neutrality, and neutrality would be enforced. Impatiently, Genêt brushed aside the warnings and went ahead outfitting privateers to attack the British. "Old Washington is jealous of my successes, and the enthusiasm with which the whole town flocks to my house," he wrote home.

Genêt exaggerated. Not the whole town flocked to his house. Philadelphia and the country were so sharply divided politically—not only over Genêt and France—that old friends crossed the street to avoid talking to Jefferson.

Jefferson stayed on into Washington's second term only at Washington's urgent request. Jefferson finally turned in his resignation on July 31, 1793. Washington got him to stay to the end of the year. One of Jefferson's last acts as Secretary of State was to send a final rebuke to Genêt, whose recall had been demanded by the United States and ordered by Paris. Then Jefferson went home.

Ironically, Genêt did not. Fearful for his own head in blood-spattered France, he stayed in the United States. Eventually, he married the daughter of New York's Governor George Clinton.

In the new year, the almonds blossomed at Monticello on March 17. That very day former Secretary of State Jefferson began planting 2400 weeping willow cuttings and the yellow jasmine.

The French Republic's minister was not called "Monsieur," but "Citizen" Genêt.

JEFFERSON AND HAMILTON

Coming to call at President Washington's mansion on Broadway one day, Jefferson found Alexander Hamilton standing dejectedly near the President's door. Jefferson had just come to New York to be Secretary of State, and he had no reason to be unfriendly to the eager Secretary of the Treasury. Hamilton was agitated and wanted to talk.

For half an hour, they paced back and forth before the President's door. The usually dapper and self-confident Hamilton explained what troubled him: the House of Representatives had defeated a bill he sponsored by two votes.

This bill provided that the federal government would take over about $21,500,000 in Revolutionary wartime debts that the states had run up on their own. The Senate had passed the measure behind closed doors, but the House had got into such an argument over it that the opposing sides—split 31 to 29—were not speaking and could not conduct any business.

Many people disliked the bill. Some states, notably Virginia, had taxed their citizens and paid part of their debts. Now their citizens would be taxed again to pay somebody else's debts, and they objected.

Hamilton was very anxious to have this bill passed because it was the first section of a much larger plan he had for reorganizing the finances of the government and of the nation as a whole. He felt that it was necessary to wipe out the nation's debts in order to begin building a sound financial reputation for America. It was important, Hamilton thought, for America to have confidence in its own financial strength, and that other countries have confidence in it as well. If American businessmen and manufacturers could trust the soundness of the government, they could expand their enterprises; they would became rich themselves and the nation would become rich. If other nations felt that American economy was sound, they would trade back and forth with Americans.

Because opposition to his program was strongest in the South, the stronghold of agrarian, non-manufacturing economy, it was natural that Hamilton should ask Jefferson, a great Southern leader, for help. Jefferson was able to see the danger in a situation where Hamilton's forces and his opponents could break the unity of the country with their arguments and debate. He agreed to discuss the situation with Hamilton at a dinner he would give—and to which he would invite a friend or two who might be helpful.

The one friend Jefferson did invite to dinner was James Madison,

Alexander Hamilton was Washington's Secretary of the Treasury from 1789 to 1795. During that time, he and Secretary of State Jefferson often disagreed over issues of finance and foreign policy. Hamilton said the anti-Federalists had a "womanish attachment to France;" but of Jefferson himself, Hamilton said: "There is no fair reason to suppose him capable of being corrupted."

In this Federalist cartoon, Washington and his troops try to head off invading French Republican "cannibals." Jefferson holds back the wheels of government.

who had become a powerful leader in Congress. Madison had worked closely with John Jay and Hamilton on the *Federalist Papers*—which had presented the case for a strong central government for the United States—but he had begun to worry about Hamilton's marked preference for certain economic groups—like the merchants and manufacturers. He also disapproved of Hamilton's open distrust of the ability of man to govern himself. Madison could see, however, that the government was much too weak and too young to survive the kind of dispute that was building up in Congress over Hamilton's financial program.

At the dinner, Jefferson, Hamilton, and Madison worked out an agreement. Jefferson would get two Virginia congressmen—Alexander White and Richard Bland Lee—to change their votes to favor Hamilton's bill for assumption, as Hamilton's plan was called. Hamilton, in return for this, agreed to modify the bill somewhat. He also agreed to support a move to have the country's permanent capital located in the South.

On the surface, Hamilton's plan to pay the country's debts was quite sound. There were, however, problems connected with it which Jefferson and Madison were not aware of when they agreed to make a deal with Hamilton. During the Revolution, the Continental Congress had run out of money. After that, it gave promissory notes to soldiers, instead of wages, and to farmers for food

half-penny 1793

penny 1793

silver dollar 1794

dime 1796

$5 gold eagle 1795

America's decimal system, on which these old coins and today's currency are based, was suggested to Congress in 1783 by Jefferson. He proposed "to adopt the Dollar as our Unit . . . and that its divisions and sub-divisions be in the decimal ratio."

and fodder. Now the new Congress would make good for the debts of the old Congress.

But many of the soldiers and farmers no longer held their notes. Word of Hamilton's plan had leaked to a few senators—friends of Hamilton—and they had told a few friends of their own. Immediately, "couriers and relay horses by land, and swift sailing pilot boats by sea, were flying in all directions," Jefferson reported. The people who had been informed ahead of time about what was going to happen in the settlement of the debt had bought the notes from the ex-soldiers and farmers, who did not know their value, at ten to fifteen per cent of their face value.

For Hamilton, his bill had an additional advantage. The government could not, for a long time, redeem the notes in money. In their place it would have to issue new, interest-bearing bonds. So the speculators (as Jefferson called them) or "stock jobbers" who obtained them would collect high interest—paid out of taxes—until they were able to cash in their high profits. Meanwhile they would support the government.

Hamilton's financial program also included the establishment of a national bank which would be called the Bank of the United States. The bank could issue paper money. Hamilton thought that by making more currency available it would aid manufacturing and trade, and encourage the development of a powerful class of merchants, manufacturers, and businessmen.

Madison soon realized what the idea behind the Bank of the United States was, and he opposed it in Congress. But he could not block the bill's passage. Washington usually took Hamilton's advice on finance just as he took Jefferson's on foreign policy, or Randolph's on law. But he had doubts about the bank

Jefferson disliked paper money, for he knew Continental dollars, like this one, had grown worthless in the Revolution.

While Jefferson was serving as Washington's Secretary of State, in Philadelphia, he lived in this pleasant house on the banks of the Schuylkill River.

bill and he asked both Hamilton and Jefferson if the Constitution permitted Congress to set up the bank?

Certainly not, said Jefferson. The Constitution says plainly what Congress' powers are. If Congress may do anything not specifically forbidden, why would the Constitution's authors have bothered to say what it *could* do? And if Congress may do anything it considers good, it could do evil, and, as the sole judge, call it good.

Certainly, said Hamilton. The Constitution, by implication, permits Congress to do anything that Congress considers good for the country, and that the Constitution does not specifically forbid.

The argument between Jefferson and Hamilton about interpretation of the Constitution is an argument which has never been settled in the government of the United States. Jefferson's position represents the "strict" interpretation of the Constitution and Hamilton's position represents what Jefferson called the "loose construction." Even today, when Congress considers a new and major bill, there are those senators and congressmen who take Jeffersonian or Hamiltonian positions as to whether or not the Constitution permits the law. It is often the function of the Supreme Court, once laws have left Congress, to make the final decision on whether or not the law is constitutional.

In the case of the Bank of the United States, Hamilton won. Washington signed the bill. Jefferson, after telling Washington that the Constitution did not give Congress the right to establish the bank, advised the President to sign the bill anyway, if in doubt, because it was the will of Congress and Congress represented the people.

Jefferson did not want a government that owed its strength to the rich. He wanted a government that represented the will of the people, all of the people. He was particularly anxious to have the rights of the nation's farmers—large and small—respected. In addition, he believed that America should remain an agricultural nation.

Neither Hamilton nor Jefferson was wholly right or wholly wrong. The country did boom while Hamilton was Secretary of the Treasury. But Hamilton did not foresee that wealth concentrated in the hands of relatively few people could endanger rather than preserve the government he served. Jefferson did not foresee a modern world in which the United States could not exist as a nation of farmers.

But Jefferson and Hamilton were not living in the future, and their differences were dividing the whole country. Most of the people were still farmers and many were ex-soldiers. They were furious when advantage was taken of them by speculators. Because of this unfair treatment they were suspicious of most of Hamilton's program, particularly his national bank.

The Bank of the United States opened its doors in Philadelphia in 1791. It closed in 1811, when Jeffersonian Democrats refused to renew its charter.

Gazette of the United States.

A NATIONAL PAPER, PUBLISHED WEDNESDAYS AND SATURDAYS BY JOHN FENNO, No. 34, NORTH FIFTH-STREET, PHILADELPHIA.

[No. 59 of Vol. IV.] SATURDAY, DECEMBER 22, 1792. [Whole No. 381.]

For the GAZETTE of the UNITED STATES.

IF perseverance can supply the want of Judgment, Mr. Jefferson has an excellent advocate in the writer of his "VINDICATION." But I mistake, if his last attempt is not found to involve still more deeply the character he wishes to extricate.

To repel the imputation on Mr. Jefferson, arising from the advice which he gave to Congress respecting the debt to France; he not only labors to shew, that taken in all its circumstances it is not of the exceptionable complexion under which it has been represented.

Now, it happens, that the variance, which is alledged to exist, if it has any influence upon the meaning of the passage, has one favorable to Mr. Jefferson; taking it for granted, that his Apologist has given a true account of it. This will be seen by carefully contrasting the phraseology in the two cases.

The extract, as stated by me, is in these words—"*If there is a danger of the public payments not being punctual*, I submit whether it may not *be better, that the discontents which would then arise, should be transferred from a Court, of whose good will we have so much need, to the breasts of a private company.*"

[...]tended to be contended for, no pains will be taken to dispute it; and the comment will be left to Mr. Jefferson's most partial admirers.

The writer of the vindication continues to insist, that Mr. Jefferson was only the vehicle of communication, assigning as reasons for this assertion that the transaction had taken place between the parties, before any mention was made of it to him, and that in communicating it to Congress he only made known to that body the desire both of the company and of the French Court; That the *opinion which he gave arose out of the proposition, was in furtherance of the*

between life and death for a time—and then as they are repugnant to rational liberty, to drop into neglect.—Doctor FRANKLIN has made some very just remarks, shewing how the desire of possessing certain finery increased the female labor that was to pay for it. His ideas have been published in most of our Gazettes, and need not be repeated. When a man takes the pains to earn money, he seems to have the best right to say how he will spend it—or if he chuses to lock it up, and not spend it at all, he has the exclusive right to do it.

What then are we to say to laws prohibiting

Fenno's newspaper, founded April 11, 1789, favored Hamilton and the Federalists.

Despite their dissatisfaction, they could not join an opposition party, because there was none. But Hamilton liked to consider himself the head of the Federalists, the name that originally belonged to all supporters of a stronger confederation of states.

The anti-Federalists, as Hamilton's supporters called his opponents, numbered an assortment of Jefferson's old friends. Patrick Henry, George Mason, and James Monroe had been opposed to Federalism all along. But Madison, Edmund Pendleton, and George Wythe, who had supported the Constitution, now were counted among the anti-Federalists.

Many of this group began to organize societies and clubs that they named not anti-Federalist, but Republican or Democratic. One, in Philadelphia, boasted Jefferson's scientist friend Dr. Rittenhouse as a founder. These people looked to Jefferson as their natural leader.

It was time, Jefferson and Madison decided, that these people had a newspaper to speak for them, and to answer the charges made by Hamilton's newspaper, the *Gazette of the United States*. Its pro-Federalist editor, a Bostonian named John Fenno, detested democracy and was attracted to monarchy. Hamilton had saved him from bankruptcy and Fenno now called him "the highest jewel in Columbia's crown."

Madison, with Jefferson's advice and help, spent a good deal of his spare time in 1791 on two projects: starting a newspaper, and organizing political opposition to Hamilton.

To edit the paper, called the *National Gazette*, Madison chose Philip Freneau, a poet who had outfitted and commanded a privateer during the Revolution. He was a devoted democrat and an ardent advocate of France's revolution. But he was reluctant to undertake the newspaper, and Jefferson made him a State Department translator at $5 a week. The job left Freneau ample time for editing.

Freneau's assault on Hamilton and his supporters in the *National Gazette* began in October, 1791 and it soon infuriated Hamilton. Hamilton lashed out at Jefferson and

National Gazette.

By P. FRENEAU: *Publiſhed* WEDNESDAYS *and* SATURDAYS, *at* THREE DOLLARS *per annum.*

[NUMB. 21 of VOL. II.] WEDNESDAY, January 9, 1793. [Total No. 125.]

To the EDITOR *of the* NATIONAL GAZETTE.

SIR,

IT is incumbent on every one who regards the intereſt and happineſs of his country, to take notice of every ſhoal and rock that have proved fatal to other republics, and endeavour to guard againſt the like miſchance in this happy land. Uned to immortal fame, received no adulation of this kind. I am as ſenſible of the ſervices of the Preſident as any man, and think him worthy of the high regard of his country. But ſurely the office he enjoys is a ſufficient teſtimony of the people's favour, without worſhipping him likewiſe. I believe, I may venture to ſay, that ſuch fulſome adulation does not accord with his feelings.

to an important public intereſt, and of having avoided the humiliation, which would have been juſtly due to an oppoſite, and to a feeble conduct.

The diſpoſition which was reſolved upon with regard to the firſt loan, involved neceſſarily a deciſion of the point, that the loans might be placed on the joint foundation of both acts. That loan having

They are therefore of no conſequence. But there are others, who ſee and judge only through the falſe medium of paſſion or prejudice, that may not reliſh theſe opinions. To them I would juſt obſerve—that the novelty of any doctrine ought not to be an argument againſt it—nor ſhould it be condemned without a fair and diſpaſſionate crimination. I appeal then to the good ſenſe of my countrymen, whether, by

Freneau's paper, begun October 31, 1791, spoke for Jefferson and the Democrats.

Freneau in letters that Fenno published. The letters bore a variety of signatures, but everybody knew Hamilton had written them. Hamilton blamed Jefferson for everything Freneau said. Actually Freneau needed no help, and probably never got any from Jefferson.

The spectacle of cabinet members squabbling in the newspapers irritated Washington. He was sixty, he had been ill, and he wanted to go home at the end of his first term in March, 1793.

Thinking toward retirement Washington began to consider candidates to succeed himself and he asked James Madison if Jefferson would take the Presidency. Madison said that Jefferson's "extreme repugnance to public life . . . made it doubtful . . ." He added that Northern prejudices against Southern leadership might bar Jefferson's election, anyway.

Hamilton and Jefferson together and, for once, in agreement, convinced Washington that he had to remain President for another term for the unity of the new nation.

Jefferson's friends, Madison and James Monroe, established a connection with George Clinton, the governor of New York. Clinton and Hamilton were contesting the political control of New York State. Hamilton had aristocratic support. Clinton was supported by Aaron Burr and Burr's Sons of St. Tammany, then a popular New York patriotic society.

The group which was called Democratic-Republican was beginning to take the shape of a second party whose members would one day call themselves Democrats.

Although Adams, the Federalist Vice-Presidential candidate supported by Hamilton, won the elections of 1792, defeating Clinton, two strong Southern states—Virginia and North Carolina—supported Clinton. The relationship between New York's urban voters and the South, powerful forces in the Democratic Party of today, had been formed. It was an alliance that eventually would take Jefferson out of retirement and send him to the White House as the nation's third President.

VICE-PRESIDENT TO JOHN ADAMS
(1797-1800)

As the stagecoach lumbered north to Philadelphia, Jefferson must have chuckled about the gift he was bringing to the American Philosophical Society, which had just elected him president to succeed the late David Rittenhouse. It was the skeleton of a monster that had once roamed western Virginia. For years afterward, Jefferson's interest in the fossil bones of ancient mastodons and mammoths was to provide material for the jokes and cartoons of Federalist editors. They called him "Mr. Mammoth" and "the Mammoth of Democracy."

Two days after his arrival in Philadelphia, on March 4, 1797, Jefferson took the oath of office as Vice-President of the United States.

This 1801 view shows Georgetown, the Potomac, and Federal City (Washington, D.C.). The government moved here from Philadelphia in 1800, during Adams' Presidency.

Three years before, when Jefferson resigned as Secretary of State and went back to Monticello, he had cancelled his newspaper subscriptions. "Politics are entirely banished from my mind," he wrote to a friend.

Jefferson's retirement was doomed, however, by the problems and real dangers that his country had to face in its struggle to remain independent and gain recognition by the other countries of the world.

Fighting France, the British had ruled the French West Indies off limits to American ships. In the 1790's captains who ignored the order found themselves shipless: the British confiscated craft, cargo, and crew. War between England and the United States threatened.

To avoid war, Washington sent Hamilton's friend John Jay to London, in 1794. The Chief Justice of the Supreme Court, Jay, was an upright patriot, but he was pro-British and lacked force. Even so, had it not been for Hamilton, he might have made a better treaty than he did.

Jay carried into the negotiations only the threat that we might put cannon aboard our merchant ships and join Sweden and Denmark in enforcing their new Armed Neutrality Convention which they had formed to protect themselves against the British. But Hamilton assured the British minister in Philadelphia that we would not do that, and Jay had to settle on Britain's terms.

The treaty that Jay agreed to repeated a British promise to quit their posts in the Northwest after June 1, 1796. The British were to be given free shipping rights on the Mississippi River. The treaty pledged the United States to pay British claims arising from the Revolution, but it did not require the British to pay claims made by the United States. It said nothing about the seizure of American ships and seamen. It did permit American ships to trade with the British West Indies, but it forbade American ships to carry to Europe any American product—cotton, sugar, rum, and molasses—which the West Indies also produced.

The Senate angrily modified the treaty before ratifying it. Even so, the agreement was a poor one, but it did avert war with Britain. At the same time, it almost got us into war with France.

Just before the storm broke, Hamilton quit as Secretary of the Treasury, but his influence on the government and Washington continued.

In 1796, the country would have to elect a President. Washington almost certainly would retire, and the way would be open for a Democratic-Republican to replace him. Jefferson wanted to stay home.

The Democratic-Republicans chose Jefferson and Aaron Burr for President and Vice-President.

Of the new Capitol building to be built in Washington, Jefferson said: "I should prefer the adoption of some one of the models of antiquity." George Washington chose instead this plan, by William Thornton, which Jefferson sketched in 1792. The building was begun in 1793. But many other architects worked on the Capitol, and its wings and present dome were not finished until 1865.

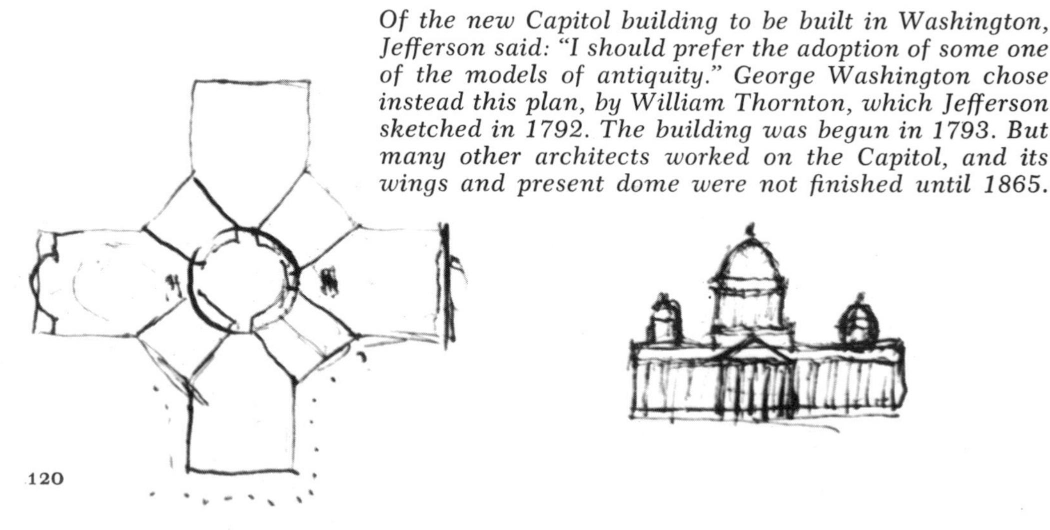

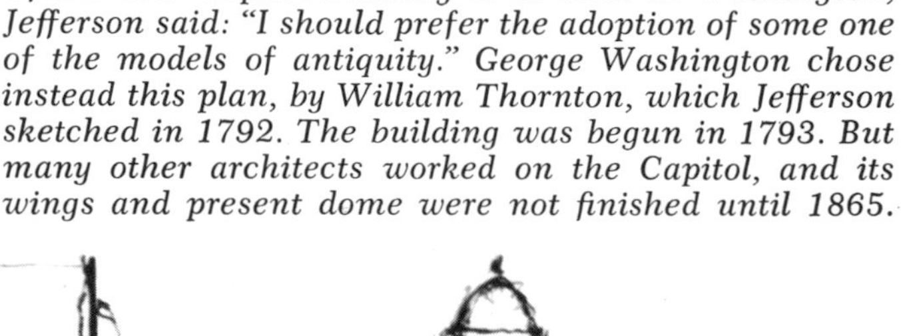

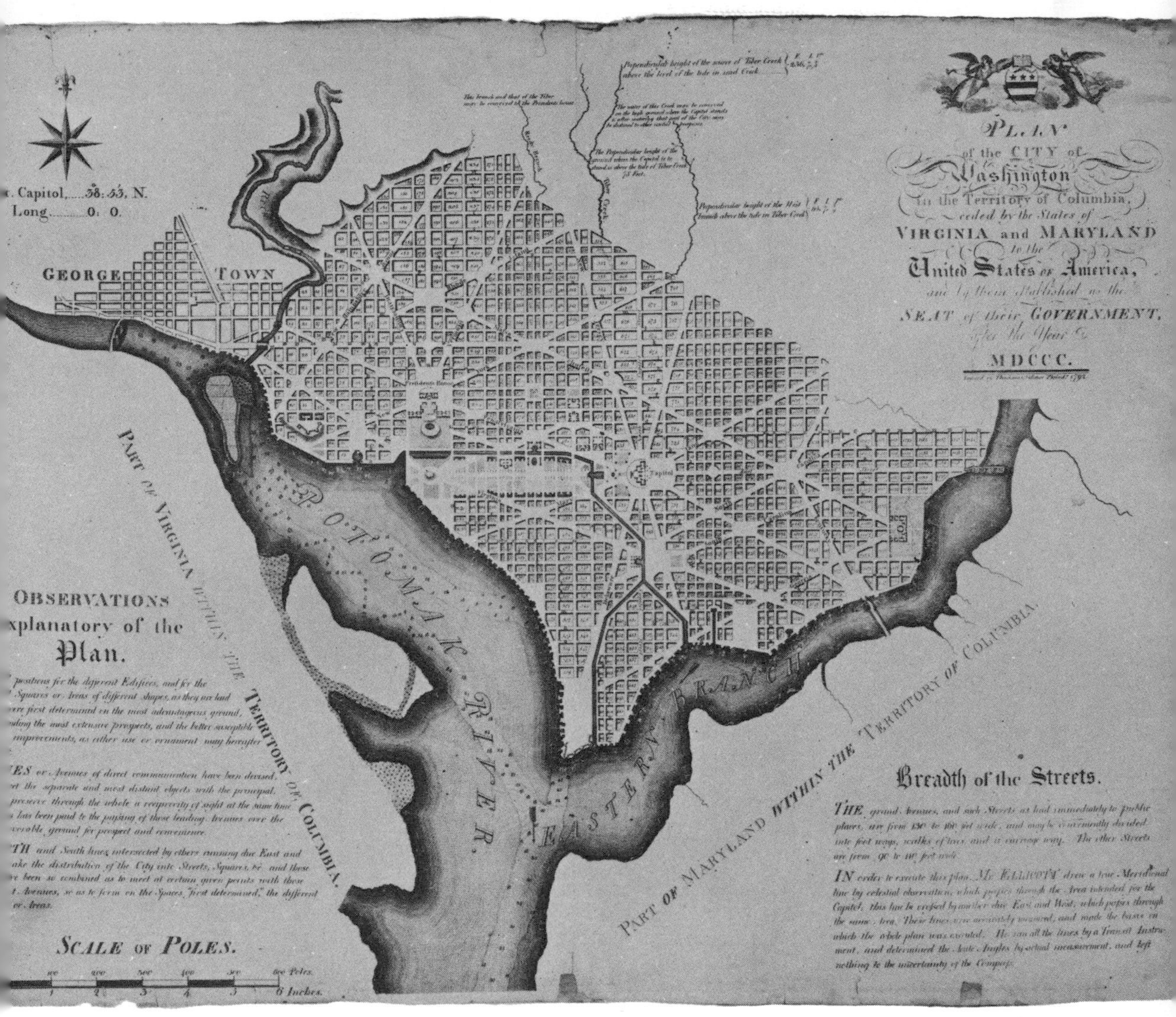

This 1792 official engraving of the proposed city of Washington shows broad avenues radiating from the Capitol—an inspiration of Pierre Charles L'Enfant, whom George Washington had asked to plan the Federal City in 1789. L'Enfant, a French army engineer, had formerly served in the American Revolutionary War.

The Federalists picked John Adams of Massachusetts for President and Thomas Pinckney of South Carolina for Vice-President.

Jefferson, who had no great desire to be President, refrained from campaigning as Adams also did. When the votes were counted in February, 1797, the results did not surprise him: Adams, 71; Jefferson, 68. He would become Vice-President, not President.

Adams called Jefferson in the day before their term began, to discuss France.

The French had been defeating Britain and Britain's allies all over Europe. They saw no need to pamper anyone who traded with the enemy, and their privateers picked off our

In 1794, Pennsylvania farmers rioted over Hamilton's tax on whiskey, and Washington (above) reviewed troops about to put down the so-called Whiskey Rebellion.

ships just as Britain's had. In this country, most Federalists spoiled for the fight. Congress voted to build a fighting fleet and fortify the coast.

John Adams was one Federalist who did not want war. He dispatched John Marshall, C. C. Pinckney, and Elbridge Gerry to Paris to try and restore friendly relations with France. In the lull which followed, Jefferson rode off to Monticello.

The news from France was bad. The mails of March, 1798, brought word that, under a new decree, France would confiscate any neutral ship carrying enemy goods. Adams replied by removing a ban on the arming of merchant ships.

Rioting erupted in Philadelphia's streets between partisans of France and partisans of Britain, and the cavalry had to stop it. Federalist newspapers imaginatively reported French troops landing in the South and French agents stirring up slaves to murder their masters.

Hamilton convinced Adams that he should recall George Washington

In 1798, during Adams's Presidency, when war threatened with France and Philadelphians rioted, Washington was called from retirement to head the army again.

to service as commander in chief of the army. Then he had Washington ask Adams to name him as second in command.

Many Federalists feared that a possible French landing would set off a rebellion by Democratic-Republicans and their foreign friends. In the national confusion, the Federalist leaders saw the chance to crush the opposition for good, and began pushing through Congress the kind of laws that pass only in hysterical times.

One law, the Alien Act, permitted the President to deport any alien he considered dangerous. The law was aimed broadly at French republicans and Irish rebels.

A companion piece to the Alien Act, was the Sedition Act, which made it a federal offense to criticize the government or its officials. A third, the Naturalization Act, made foreigners wait fourteen years for citizenship. The bills passed not only because the Federalists were frightened, but because some Demo-

In this cartoon, an eagle prevents Jefferson from burning the Constitution on the Altar of Gallic (French) Despotism.

cratic-Republicans feared they would be considered unpatriotic if they opposed them.

Fear of the Alien Act sent two shiploads of Frenchmen hurrying back to Europe. In London, our Minister, Rufus King, asked the British not to exile to America any more Irish rebels against George III.

When John Taylor suggested that Virginia and North Carolina ought to secede from the union in protest against the acts, Jefferson counseled "a little patience and we shall see the reign of witches pass over, their spells dissolved and the people recovering their true sight."

As Vice-President, he could not do much about the Alien and Sedition Acts. As political leader of the Democratic-Republicans he did a great deal. He wrote tirelessly to people all over the country. Jefferson struck out at all of the policies the Federalists had come to stand for.

In the privacy of Monticello, Jefferson worked on an important document. This document was aimed at the Alien and Sedition Acts. It argued that since the states had created the federal government, they had the right to challenge federal laws they thought unconstitutional.

John Breckenridge presented Jefferson's document to the Kentucky legislature under his own name. Similar but milder resolutions, drawn by Madison, were presented in Virginia. These Kentucky and Virginia Resolutions quickly passed the vote of their state legislatures, and were sent to other states.

Long after Jefferson died, defenders of the slavery that he detested extended his arguments to the point of secession, and as a result plunged the nation into the Civil War. But at the time, Jefferson was protesting against the restrictions of human freedom under the Alien and Sedition Acts.

A campaign poster for the year 1800.

REPUBLICANS

Turn out, turn out and save your Country from ruin!

From an *Emperor*—from a *King*—from the iron grasp of a *British Tory Faction*—an unprincipled banditti of British speculators. The hireling tools and emissaries of his majesty king George the 3d have thronged our city and diffused the poison of principles among us.

DOWN WITH THE TORIES, DOWN WITH THE BRITISH FACTION,

Before they have it in their power to enslave you, and reduce your families to distress by heavy taxation. Republicans want no Tribute-liars—they want no ship Ocean-liars—they want no Rufus King's for Lords—they want no Varick to lord it over them—they want no Jones for senator, who fought with the British against the Americans in time of the war.—But they want in their places such men as

Jefferson & Clinton,

who fought their Country's Battles in the year '76

One day, after months of fuming and suspicion, John Adams became aware of what his position in the government really was. Ever since he had assumed office, another man, Alexander Hamilton, had really been President, writing secret letters and giving secret orders to Adams' Cabinet. It had taken Adams a long time to realize what Hamilton had been doing, but when he did, he acted at once. He ordered a peace mission to depart for France by the end of the month. Adams never regretted his brave behavior but he had shattered his party. The party was divided between Hamiltonians and Adamsites. George Washington died at Mount Vernon on December 14, 1799, and the Federalists no longer could use his great prestige for their own purposes.

It was not until the next spring that a caucus of Democratic-Republican congressmen formally named Jefferson and Burr the party's candidates in the 1800 Presidential election, but Jefferson was already assured of being the candidate by the beginning of the new year.

It was a curious and bitter campaign year. The Federalists, split but still fighting, pictured Jefferson as a scoundrel, a ruffian, a thief, a coward, and an infidel.

Home at Monticello throughout the campaign, Jefferson made no speeches and tried to keep his temper.

Twice during the year personal affairs saddened him: his long-time servant and friend Jupiter, and his daughter Maria's baby both died. But during the campaign he seemed serene. Jefferson was a genius as a political organizer, and his lieutenants had constructed a smooth-running political machine.

Jefferson was criticized when his friend, the revolutionary Tom Paine, published a letter attacking George Washington in 1796.

Adams made conservative John Marshall Chief Justice of the Supreme Court just before he left the Presidency in 1801.

Jefferson was in Washington when the election returns began coming in. Still a swampy village, Washington had become the nation's capital in June, and Jefferson, still Vice-President, arrived late in November to preside over the Senate.

With the election returns, came congratulations. Jefferson and Burr, with 73 electoral votes each, had beaten Adams with 65 and Pinckney with 64. But the tie between Jefferson and Burr meant the House of Representatives would have to choose the President.

During Jefferson's Vice-Presidency an undeclared naval war broke out with France. Here, the American frigate, Constellation, *captures the French ship,* L'Insurgente, *off Guadeloupe in 1799.*

When the House of Representatives met in Washington on February 11 to choose a President, eight of the sixteen states were for Jefferson, six for Burr, and two undecided. Each state had one vote, and nine votes were needed to elect. Nineteen times that day, and far into the night, the House voted, but the vote never changed.

The political bitterness grew dangerous. Against Hamilton's advice the Federalists had supported Burr, but the more moderate ones began to worry: were they endangering the union? At length, when some of them withheld their votes, Maryland and Vermont switched to Jefferson on the thirty-sixth ballot. He had ten votes. He had been elected.

The night of March 3, John Adams prepared an unpleasant legacy for his successor. The Federalist Congress had created a number of additional judgeships and Adams had appointed Federalist politicians to the posts. Their futures were assured. But as Adams' term neared its end, not all the commissions had yet been issued, and John Marshall, whom Adams had named Chief Justice, but who was still serving as Secretary of State, sat far into the night signing them. Vice-President Jefferson knew what was happening. He called in Levi Lincoln, who was going to be his Attorney General, gave him his watch, and told him to take over the State Department at midnight.

At the stroke of twelve, Lincoln strode into Marshall's office and said: "I have been ordered by Mr. Jefferson to take possession of this office and its papers."

Marshall, looking at his watch, and at the unsigned commissions on his desk, protested that Jefferson was not yet President because it was not yet twelve o'clock.

"This is the President's watch," said Lincoln, showing Jefferson's. "It rules the hour." A number of the commissions stayed on the desk, undelivered, and Marshall sheepishly departed. But he did have a few of the documents in his pocket signed, and the men who received them were thereafter called "John Adams' Midnight Judges."

On March 4, 1801, Thomas Jefferson was inaugurated in Washington as the third President of the United States. His old friend John Adams did not attend the ceremony.

In 1802, as President, Jefferson was sketched by artist Benjamin Latrobe.

THE "REVOLUTION OF 1800" (1800-1809)

Thomas Jefferson, third President of the United States, seated on the floor of the Executive Mansion, was romping with his grandchildren—"playing the fool," he said. Walking in on the scene, Baron Alexander von Humboldt, a visiting German scientist, was not surprised. What did shock von Humboldt was a Federalist newspaper that he found, another day, on the table in the President's study. It was so full of outrageous lies about Mr. Jefferson that von Humboldt asked why the President had not suppressed the paper and jailed the editor.

Jefferson grinned. "Put that paper in your pocket, Baron," he said, "and should you hear the reality of our liberty, the freedom of the press questioned, show them this paper—and tell them where you found it."

On Inauguration Day, March 4, the nation celebrated its happiest holiday since the peace with Britain in 1783. Outside of the boarding house in Washington, where Jefferson lived, a crowd was waiting.

Toward ten o'clock, militia from Alexandria began parading, but Jefferson chatted quietly with friends. A little before noon, he walked with them to the Capitol, where Aaron Burr, Chief Justice Marshall, and members of the Senate and House of Representatives awaited him.

In a gentle voice that could barely be heard in the little crowded chamber, Jefferson extended a friendly hand to his foes. He told them: "We are all Republicans, we are all Federalists. . . ."

Despite his gentle words, Jefferson considered his election a revolution, a revolution as important as that of 1776. The country was a quarter of a century old, and it had yet to become the kind of country he had hoped for when he wrote the Declaration of Independence. Now, Jefferson was determined, it would.

Jefferson quickly pardoned everyone imprisoned under the Sedition

Act, returned their fines, and sent them personal letters apologizing for their persecution. He had the new Congress, which was on his side, get rid of the "Midnight Judges."

Deftly, Jefferson outwitted the people who wanted to preserve in the Executive Mansion the atmosphere of a royal court. Anyone could visit him almost any time, but he abolished the stuffy levees or receptions at which, once a week, Washington and Adams had greeted long lines of elegant visitors.

He took to wearing shoes with laces—an innovation widely remarked—because he considered buckles foppish and undemocratic. He casually received the British minister, Anthony Merry, in bedroom slippers.

The President forbade the use of his face on coins. He forbade celebration of his birthday, and to make sure that nobody violated the rule, he would not even tell anyone the date.

On New Year's Day and the Fourth of July, everybody came to the President's house: diplomats and drovers, counts and clerks, and Jefferson mingled with them all. At the first such party—July 4, 1801—early callers found him chatting with five Cherokee chiefs. The Indians considered him their friend, and he was still busily studying Indian languages.

When Patsy and Polly and his grandchildren were not with him, he enjoyed the company of his two mockingbirds—which flew freely in and out of a cage surrounded by roses and geraniums. One, his favorite, ate from his lips and could imitate any bird it ever had heard. When Jefferson wanted a nap, the bird hopped up the stairs behind him, then perched on his shoulder and sang to him as he dozed.

Jefferson had named an excellent cabinet: Albert Gallatin was Secretary of the Treasury, and Madison Secretary of State. The President and his aides cut the Navy to size, called home unnecessary diplomats, and abolished unnecessary government jobs. With the savings, they repealed all internal taxes and at the same time began paying government debts which were a legacy from Hamilton's regime.

In office only a few weeks, the new government boldly took on a war. For a long time, to Jefferson's annoyance, our government, like other

Dolly Madison was Jefferson's hostess when his daughter Martha (Mrs. T. M. Randolph, below) was not in Washington.

The squadron of ships Jefferson sent to blockade Tripoli was commanded by Captain Edward Preble. One frigate—Bainbridge's Philadelphia*—was captured by the Tripolitans who imprisoned the American sailors, and put their own crew aboard.*

One of Preble's men—Stephen Decatur—suggested sailing the ketch Intrepid (*at left*) *into the harbor, and setting the* Philadelphia *afire. The feat took place in February, 1804, but Tripoli continued to molest American shipping until 1805.*

Aaron Burr was Vice-President during Jefferson's first term as President.

governments, had been paying the piratical Arab rulers of North Africa to leave merchant ships alone. When Jefferson became President, the Pasha of Tripoli demanded an increase in his annual $80,000 bribe. Rebuffed, he declared war on the United States on May 14, 1801. Jefferson promptly dispatched a squadron of ships to blockade Tripoli.

But Jefferson had far more important powers to deal with than the pirates of Barbary. Ever since 1762, Spain had owned the former French territory of Louisiana—almost a million square miles of forests, plains, mountains, and river valleys.

The Mississippi River was the boundary between this territory and the United States, and the city of New Orleans, at the river's mouth, was the territory's gate. Americans living inland, away from the Atlantic, shipped their goods down the Mississippi to New Orleans, where they enjoyed the "right of deposit," that is, they could store their goods there untaxed, to be put aboard ship.

The Louisiana territory and the country beyond it had tantalized Jefferson for a long time. Always seeking to know the unknown, he had urged the American Philosophical Society—way back in 1792—to send an exploration party across the continent and he had offered to contribute to the cost. Meriwether Lewis, a nineteen-year-old neighbor of Jefferson's, had volunteered for the proposed 1792 expedition. The expedition fell through but Jefferson had kept in touch with Lewis and, as President, had Lewis, now an army captain, as his secretary.

Shocking news about that wonderful world came little more than a month after Jefferson's inauguration, and even before the Pasha's declaration of war: Spain had secretly ceded Louisiana to France.

As long as Spain was our neighbor, we had had little to worry about. Spain, as a lesser power, was no threat. France was. Under the ambitious Napoleon Bonaparte, who had become First Consul, France had become dangerously powerful and warlike. Some Federalists agitated for war with France.

Some Democratic - Republicans joined in the clamor after the Spanish governor of New Orleans, and then Napoleon himself, canceled the "right of deposit" for American shipping on the Mississippi.

The closing of the port of New Orleans to American goods and the abrupt end of the "right of deposit" disturbed many Americans. It angered the farmers of Kentucky and Tennessee who depended upon the Mississippi River and the duty-free port of New Orleans for shipping their produce. These farmers had always been loyal supporters of Jefferson but there was a good chance that they would switch their support to Burr if Jefferson did not do something to open up the river.

Hamilton used these pistols in the duel in which he was killed by Burr in 1804.

This Federalist cartoon claimed that Jefferson was destroying the government.

MAD TOM in A RAGE

Jefferson sat down with Madison and Monroe and decided that we should try to buy New Orleans and West Florida from the French for ten million dollars, which Congress quietly voted. If the French refused to sell, we should seek an agreement on freely using the port. If that failed, we should negotiate secretly for an alliance with Britain.

But our minister in France, Robert R. Livingston, spoke French clumsily. Somewhat deaf, he understood it no better. When Talleyrand, who was France's foreign minister, hinted that he might be willing to accept a bribe, the upright Livingston ignored him. Talleyrand finally brushed off Livingston's offer to buy New Orleans.

Just before Monroe arrived in France to help Livingston, however, Napoleon decided upon war with Britain. Napoleon knew that if he fought Britain, the British fleet could quickly capture New Orleans; without New Orleans, the Louisiana territory would be worthless to France.

Talleyrand offered all of Louisiana to Livingston. Next day Monroe arrived in Paris. The two envoys had neither the money nor the authority to close so tremendous and astonishing a deal, but boldly and sensibly, they went ahead on their own, haggled and bargained, got the price down to $15,000,000, and signed the treaty May 2, 1803. The Louisiana territory was ours.

The United States paid about three cents an acre for the land of the Louisiana Territory. The unusually low price did not prevent the Senate, with Federalists in the lead, from protesting the treaty both in regard to money—$15,000,000 was a lot of money no matter what was bought with it—and in regard to the United States Constitution. The treaty had had to be kept secret and had been signed without the advice and cooperation of Congress. Jefferson answered the protests about money by saying that the land could be sold to settlers. Supporters of the treaty agreed that it was not strictly constitutional but that, in the long run, the best interests of the American people had been served. The Senate ratified the treaty buying the Louisiana Territory by a vote of twenty-four to seven.

Months before Talleyrand's surprising offer, Jefferson's scientific curiosity about the Louisiana Terri-

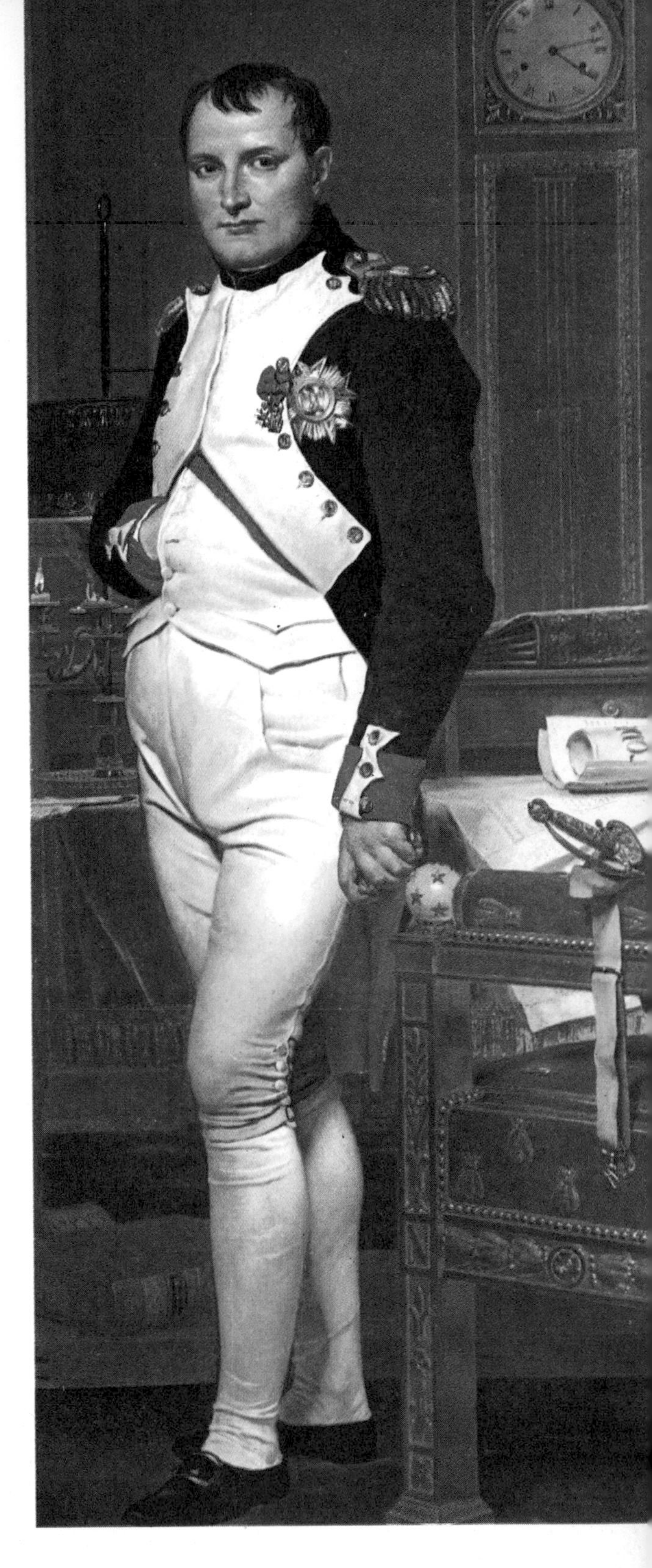

Since Napoleon (right), First Consul of France, needed money for his European wars, he decided to sell all Louisiana to the United States. The scene at left shows the raising of the American flag over New Orleans on December 20, 1803.

THE LOUISIANA PURCHASE

Doubled the size of the United States with the addition of 828,000 square miles of territory.

tory had overcome him. With the secret approval of Congress—secret because France still owned Louisiana—Jefferson ordered Meriwether Lewis to undertake the exploration that they had often talked about.

Lewis selected as his companion, William Clark, youngest brother of George Rogers Clark, and an old comrade-in-arms of his own. The Indians called him "Red Head."

The major objective of the expedition was to explore the Missouri River and determine how easily the continent could be crossed by this route. But along the way the party would study every aspect of the land—its soil, its climate, its plant and animal life. Beneath the soil, the explorers would seek out fossil bones and mineral riches. They would offer friendship, trade, education, and even vaccination to the Indians, and they would study every aspect of Indian life—their tribal names, their numbers, their languages, laws, and traditions.

Three boats bearing Lewis, Clark, soldiers, civilians, an interpreter, and Clark's Negro servant York—43 persons in all—headed up the Missouri from St. Louis on May 14, 1804, and covered 1,400 miles before settling down to winter with the Mandan Indians in what is now North Dakota. The temperature dropped to 43 degrees below zero, Fahrenheit. With spring, the party pushed further up the Missouri, then along a tributary—which Lewis christened the Jefferson River—into Shoshone territory in what is now Montana. The Shoshones contributed horses for the crossing of the Rockies; then the explorers paddled down the Columbia, sighting the Pacific on November 15, 1805.

Even before Lewis and Clark returned—they reached St. Louis in September, 1806—Jefferson sent the dashing Lieutenant Zebulon Pike off on another expedition: Pike explored the headwaters of the Mississippi (1805–1806), and explored the headwaters of the Arkansas and Red Rivers (1806–1807). During the last phase of his expedition he discovered the peak in Colorado that is now known as Pike's Peak.

They were great days. For Jefferson they should have been his happiest. But Polly—the beautiful Maria—had not been feeling well after the birth of her second child, a girl also named Maria.

The good, kind Patsy, who had children of her own to tend, brought her sister to her own home at Edgehill, near Shadwell, to care for her and her baby. But Polly faded. Jefferson, stopping at Edgehill on his way to Monticello for a spring visit, thought she might do better on the mountaintop, and had his men bear her four miles on a stretcher to her childhood home. There, on mild sunny days, they used to take her for a gentle ride around the gardens, with men instead of horses drawing the carriage. Nothing helped. Polly died on April 17, 1804.

The day Polly died, Jefferson hid himself for hours. A little later, he wrote to his old friend John Page, now governor of Virginia:

"Others may lose of their abundance, but I, of my want, have lost even the half of all I had."

Abigail Adams—who had not spoken or written to Jefferson since his split with her husband—grieved too. The little girl who had visited her in England had won a permanent place in her heart. Abigail wrote a comforting note, and Jefferson, sending his thanks, intimated that old friends ought not to stay angry at each other. Jefferson chose to forget his disputes with Adams over the form the American government should take—Adams had wanted it to be too much like the British monarchy for Jefferson's taste—and hoped Adams would forget, too.

In the Presidential elections of 1804, Jefferson got the vote of the electors of fifteen of the seventeen states.

Jefferson's second term as President was a troubled time for the country. He was blamed for much of the unpleasantness in national politics and in the dealings of the United States with other countries; the Federalists and the merchant captains of New England were particularly strong in their criticism.

Exploring the west for President Jefferson, Lewis and Clark's party met a band of friendly Flathead Indians at Ross's Hole, Montana, on September 4, 1805.

One unpleasantness involved Aaron Burr. While Burr was still Vice-President — during Jefferson's first term—Hamilton's and Burr's bad feeling for each other led Burr to the point where he challenged Hamilton to a duel and killed him. Burr—indicted for murder—fled New York and began wandering the country. His political career was completely finished.

In 1807 Americans and Britons exchanged gunfire. This fight had begun smouldering when the British man-of-war *Leopard* put into Norfolk in June and some of her crew deserted. Determined to get the deserters, and convinced that they had signed aboard the American frigate *Chesapeake*, the British captain sailed his craft just beyond the three-mile limit and waited. When the *Chesapeake* came out, he demanded the deserters. The *Chesapeake*, though most of her guns were out of commission, refused. The *Leopard* fired away. After the *Chesapeake* had suffered twenty-one casualties, she surrendered. The British boarded, took off four men, and departed.

Then both vessels sailed peaceably back to Hampton Roads.

Jefferson demanded an apology from Britain, failed to get it, and ordered British warships barred from American ports. A great many angry people wanted to do much more; they boycotted British goods and once again war seemed inevitable.

Actually, there was more cause for war than the *Chesapeake* incident. Britain and France, at each other's throats again, had declared mutual blockades, and were seizing neutral ships, including ours, that carried goods destined for the enemy. The British were worse than the French because they had more warships to

Meriwether Lewis

William Clark

On their journey, Lewis and Clark were the first Americans to see grizzly bears.

enforce their decrees, and because they insisted on searching American vessels for their own deserters.

Jefferson hurriedly ordered construction of a fleet of gunboats which his critics considered a great joke. But he still opposed war—if it could be avoided honorably—and he figured out a plan. Jefferson convinced Congress to pass an Embargo Act forbidding export of American products. We simply would not trade with other nations. Nobody would bother our ships because none of our ships would be at sea. Jefferson reasoned that, deprived of American wheat, cotton, and tobacco, the warring powers would soon have to come to terms with us.

As a result of the Embargo Act, the prices of wheat, cotton, and tobacco dropped rapidly. Hungry sailors and idle ships crowded our ports, and warehouses stood empty and silent. All over the East, people muttered unhappily against Jefferson's folly. It seemed, at first, as though only smugglers thrived, and the French and the British managed without us.

But because imports as well as exports had halted, manufacturing boomed: textile mills, potteries, foundries, hat makers, sprang up. Farmers who could not sell their crops moved to town and took factory jobs. Jefferson still believed in a democracy of small farmers, but he was a practical man and he wrote to Lafayette: "Our Embargo has produced one very happy permanent effect. It has set us all on domestic manufactures, and will, I verily believe, reduce our future demands on England fully one half."

And for a few precious years it did keep us out of a war that could only have been fruitless.

This Mandan Indian returned with Lewis and Clark from their western trip in 1806.

Despite the discontents provoked by the Embargo Act, Jefferson could probably have been elected to a third term: the Jeffersonians far outnumbered the die-hard Federalists. But Jefferson had always regretted that the Constitution did not limit a President's time in office. He still feared an attempt to make the Presidency a lifetime affair. So, long before March 4, 1809, he had been looking to retirement and he had sponsored James Madison to succeed him.

Thomas Jefferson's last day in the Presidency dawned bright. Washington was jammed; thousands of gay folk crowded the route from Madison's house to the Capitol. An escort of infantry and cavalry awaited Mr. Jefferson. When he saw the troops, he waved a salute, touched his horse's flank with his heel, and with only his grandson Jefferson Randolph—Patsy's son—by his side, he rode off. At the Capitol he tied his horse to the fence and went in to see Madison inaugurated.

At the White House, the fossil bones were packed for shipment to Monticello; so were pounds and pounds of notes on Indian languages.

Jefferson rode home to Monticello in a blinding snowstorm. He was a happy man. He could say, with pardonable pride: "I have the consolation to reflect that during the period of my administration not a drop of the blood of a single fellow citizen was shed by the sword of war or of the law."

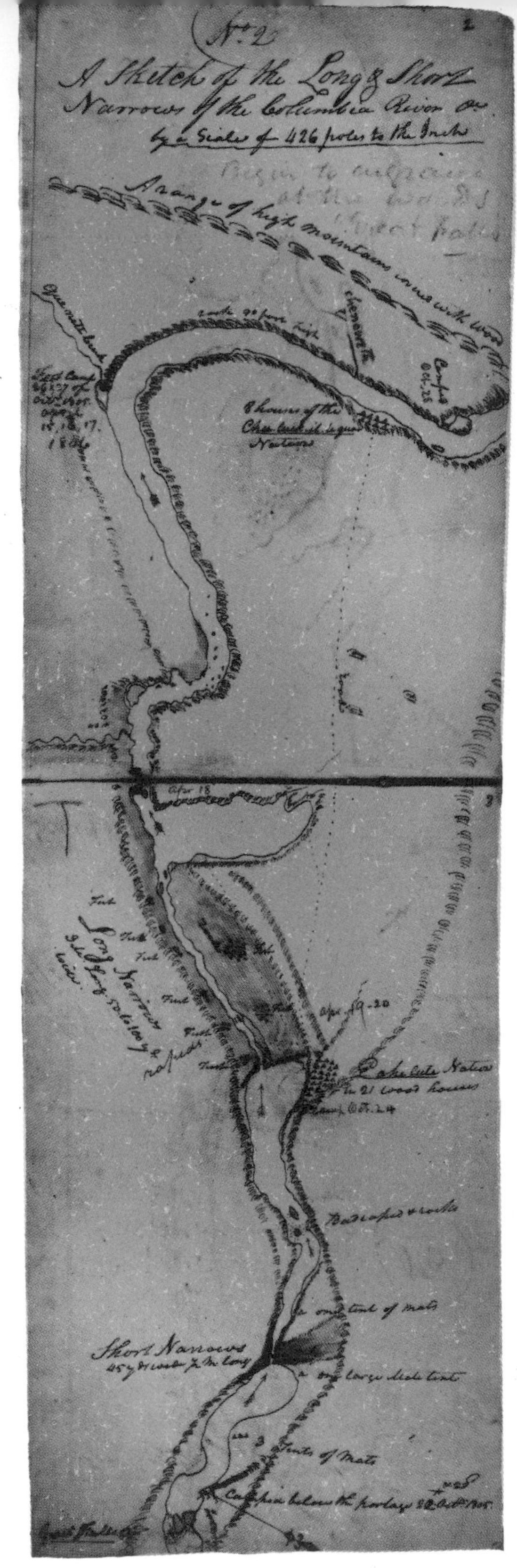

Lewis and Clark brought back notebooks and journals containing sketches, such as this map of the Columbia River narrows.

THE SAGE OF MONTICELLO
(1809-1826)

Rearranging his beloved books on the shelves of his library at Monticello, Mr. Jefferson hummed a tune that he recalled from his youth at William and Mary.

Now, at last, he wrote to his old friend General Thaddeus Kosciusko—the Polish soldier who helped lead American troops in the Revolution—that he could "enjoy a repose to which I have long been a stranger." Nobody else would have called it repose. He was as busy—by his own description—"as a bee in a molasses barrel."

Almost everything he tackled, he improved. Surveying his orchards and forests, he awed his overseer by knowing the name of every tree, and demanding what had become of any one that was missing. Rather than chop down trees for fence rails, he

This watercolor of Monticello—perhaps by a member of Jefferson's immediate family—was done in 1826, the year Jefferson, "The Sage of Monticello," died.

had living fences of thorn bushes planted.

He devised a collapsible leather top, not unlike those on modern convertible cars, to keep off the rain. He made his house more efficient with a dumb-waiter which could bring up wine from his cellar.

As an inventor, Jefferson sought no profits: writing to Charles Willson Peale, the artist, that he was sending him a mouldboard, Jefferson told him he was free to copy it if he wished, for Jefferson had "never thought of monopolizing by patent any useful idea which happens to offer itself to me."

As many as 1,300 letters a year—hundreds of them asking favors—deluged Jefferson, and he tried to answer them all. Ever since his accident in Paris, when he had injured his right wrist, he had been able to write with either hand, but even so, he could not keep up with his mail. That was how he came to adopt the polygraph, which permitted him to write several identical letters at once.

Guests were as bad as letter writers. As many as fifty showed up in a day and Patsy, keeping house for her father, had to provide the beds and meals for them. They came from everywhere in the United States. A judge arrived with a letter of introduction and stayed three weeks. An acquaintance from Europe brought his family of six and stayed ten months.

Jefferson's hospitality and the effects of events in Europe were driving him to bankruptcy. His farms were producing as never before, but war in Europe—Napoleon had overrun the whole continent—kept him from selling his wheat and tobacco. By 1814, he was desperately in need of money.

The solution that Jefferson found for his problem was, characteristically, one that enriched his country. When the British, in the War of 1812, burned the Capitol and the Executive Mansion on August 25, 1814, they destroyed some books that Congress had collected. So Jefferson offered to Congress his magnificent library with its 10,000 volumes on history, zoology, medicine, agriculture, chemistry, physics, astronomy, mathematics, religion, law, politics, philosophy, and a dozen other sciences. Thus was born the Library of Congress, one of the world's greatest collections of knowledge. The $23,950 that Congress paid Jefferson did not last long: $15,000 went at once to pay debts. And despite his difficulties, Jefferson began buying more books—as he said he could not live without them.

Jefferson and Adams had long wanted to become friends once more. Mutual friends reported Jefferson's good feelings to Adams. In 1812 they began the fascinating correspondence which continued for the rest of their lives.

The old passions were indeed dead. Jefferson had installed a bust of Hamilton in a place of honor in the salon at Monticello.

One dream, one ambition that Jefferson never abandoned, centered on a great public educational system for Virginia, complete from primary grades to university. A friend of Jefferson, a young invalid named Joseph C. Cabell, was devoting his life to battling in the legislature for educational ideas like Jefferson's, but nothing seemed to happen.

Then, one day in 1814, Jefferson was out riding when his nephew, Peter Carr, hailed him.

Peter, Dabney Carr's son, was presiding over the board of directors of a small private school near Monticello. The directors of the school, Carr told him, were in need of Jefferson's advice.

This engraving of the University of Virginia was made in 1824, when 81-year-old Jefferson was supervising the construction of the buildings he had designed.

Out of Jefferson's conversation with the directors, grew a decision to transform the little academy into a college, without state help. Jefferson, though he was deep in debt, contributed $1,000 toward the college building program.

When Central College neared completion, Jefferson made his next move. He drew up "A Bill for Establishing a System of Public Education." Joseph Cabell introduced it and got the legislature to vote $45,000 for public schools, and $15,000 for a state university.

Jefferson knew where he wanted the University to be. It was going to be where he could keep his eye on it, in Charlottesville, close to Monticello. At a private conference with him on the hilltop, his old friends, former President Madison and President James Monroe, agreed. They were all members of the twenty-four-man commission the legislature had chosen to make the final decision.

Every region of Virginia had a claim to present. But Jefferson was overwhelmingly armed.

The University should be in a healthful place, should it not? Jefferson produced a long list of men over eighty years old who lived in or around Charlottesville.

The university should be centrally situated, should it not? Jefferson produced a cardboard cut-out map of Virginia and spun it on the point of an upright pencil. The map balanced where the pencil point touched the dot that signified Charlottesville, Jefferson's chosen site.

But perhaps Charlottesville was not the center of population? Jefferson produced a cardboard map with the population figures for every county. Charlottesville was indeed the center of population.

For any remaining doubters, Jefferson had a clincher. Central College was almost finished. Jefferson was able to offer it to the state as part of the new university.

Jefferson loved Virginia's dogwood, and the marvelous songs of her mockingbirds.

Jefferson won. He got even more than he had asked. "This is Mr. Jefferson's scheme," said Madison. "It is but fair that he should carry it out in his own way."

Jefferson the architect promptly went to work drafting plans for handsome, domed, and columned buildings. Jefferson the surveyor measured off the sites with pegs and a ball of twine. Jefferson the engineer calculated the amount of brick and stone and lumber needed. Jefferson the building contractor hired bricklayers and carpenters, and imported sculptors from Italy.

In 1825, Lafayette returned to the United States, and paid a visit to his 82-year-old friend Jefferson, at Monticello.

Jefferson the educator dispatched a scholarly scout to Oxford, Cambridge, and Edinburgh to recruit great teachers, for what the university would teach concerned Jefferson even more than its appearance.

Every workday, he rode the four miles down the hill to Charlottesville on Eagle, his horse, riding about the building site, supervising everything. When he was not on the spot, through his telescope in the garden he watched the work's progress at Monticello.

The University of Virginia opened its doors on March 5, 1825. It would serve, Jefferson wrote, "for the instruction of those who are to come after us." He added, "I hope its influence on their virtue, freedom, fame and happiness, will be salutary and permanent."

One day in October, 1823, Jefferson had opened a letter from President Monroe which contained astonishing news. Foreign Minister George Canning of Britain had intelligence that Russia, Prussia, Spain, Austria, and France were going to try to recapture newly independent South America. That was not so surprising: The shock lay in a question Canning asked of Monroe. Would the United States be interested, Canning wanted to know, in cooperating with Britain to prevent the scheme from succeeding.

It was a startling suggestion. For half a century America had been at odds with Britain, and less than a decade before, had fought her for the second time. What, Monroe asked, did Jefferson advise?

Jefferson responded almost at once. The United States should agree to Canning's offer at once. And we should be guided in our foreign policy by a determination to keep out of Europe's affairs, and to keep Europe out of our affairs. Monroe took Jefferson's advice.

The Monroe Doctrine, which resulted, stated the attitude of the United States toward the young republics of Latin America for Jefferson's time and it is still in effect today. There was to be no more European colonization in Latin America. The United States and the Latin American countries would live together as equal partners—one American country would not interfere in the politics of another. Although the military strength of the United States was not great enough to enforce the Doctrine for many years, the new cooperation with Great Britain put the great force of the British navy behind it.

In 1821, when he was seventy-nine, he took time out from the labors on the university to visit the Natural Bridge in Rockbridge County. Home again, he wrote: "I was six days successively on horseback from breakfast to sunset." The next year he tripped on a rotten board on the terrace of Monticello, and broke his left arm near the wrist. The right arm had been troubling him, too, and he was never able to use either arm freely again.

President Madison (above) and President Monroe frequently consulted Thomas Jefferson during their terms of office.

The year Jefferson was 82, Lafayette came to Monticello. The two old friends had corresponded but they had not seen one another for thirty-six years. "As Lafayette descended from the carriage," Thomas Jefferson Randolph remembered, "Jefferson descended the steps of the portico . . . Jefferson was feeble and tottering with age—Lafayette perma-

These insects were painted by Benjamin Latrobe, on a journey through Virginia.

nently lamed and broken in health . . . As they approached each other, their uncertain gait quickened itself into a shuffling run, and exclaiming, 'Ah, Jefferson!' 'Ah, Lafayette!' they burst into tears as they fell into each other's arms."

Jefferson had always had trouble with finances, although he had been a wealthy man at some points in his life. By 1826 his generosity to friends and his old debts had placed him in serious financial trouble. He wrote to Madison that he would have to ask legislative permission to sell some of his beloved lands by lottery. Word of Jefferson's trouble shocked America. Before the Virginia legislature could vote its permission for the lottery, mass meetings all over the country rallied to Jefferson's aid. In New York City, $8,500 was quickly collected, in Philadelphia, $5,000, in Baltimore $3,000. Gratefully, Jefferson accepted "the pure and unsolicited offering of love."

For several years Jefferson had been ill. By March of 1826, he knew that the end could not be far, and calmly drew his will. He bequeathed Monticello to Martha and her children, more distant lands in Bedford County to his grandson Francis Eppes, a gold watch to each of his grandchildren, a walking stick to "my friend James Madison," and his new library to the University of Virginia. He gave cabins, the tools of their trades, and freedom to his favorite slaves.

In mid-June, for the first time in his life, he was confined to his bed. Regretfully, he declined an invitation to go to Washington for the celebration of the fiftieth anniversary of the Declaration of Independence. By the second of July he was fading fast, but was desperately eager to linger until the Fourth.

His mind wandered to the heroic past, to the days just before the Revolution. "Warn the Committee of Safety," he commanded. About 7 P.M. of July 3, 1826, he asked his physician "Is it the Fourth?" and the doctor comforted him: "It soon will be."

Next day, all over the country, guns boomed, bells rang, and voices rose in song to celebrate the country's fiftieth Fourth of July. The uproar was at its loudest at noon. At 12:50 P.M., Thomas Jefferson died on his peaceful Virginia hilltop.

Far away, in Massachusetts, John Adams, too, lay dying on this Fourth of July. As though defying whatever evil might threaten America, he spoke his last words: "Thomas Jefferson still survives."

In 1826, Jefferson was so poor he had to sell lottery tickets for money to keep from losing his beloved home, Monticello.

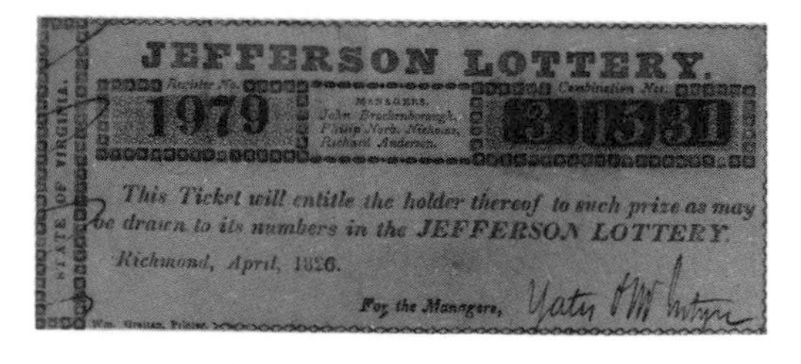

STATE OF VIRGINIA.

JEFFERSON LOTTERY.

Register No. 1979

MANAGERS.
John Brockenbrough,
Philip Norb. Nicholas,
Richard Anderson.

Combination No. 3 15 31

This Ticket will entitle the holder thereof to such prize as may be drawn to its numbers in the JEFFERSON LOTTERY.

Richmond, April, 1826.

For the Managers,

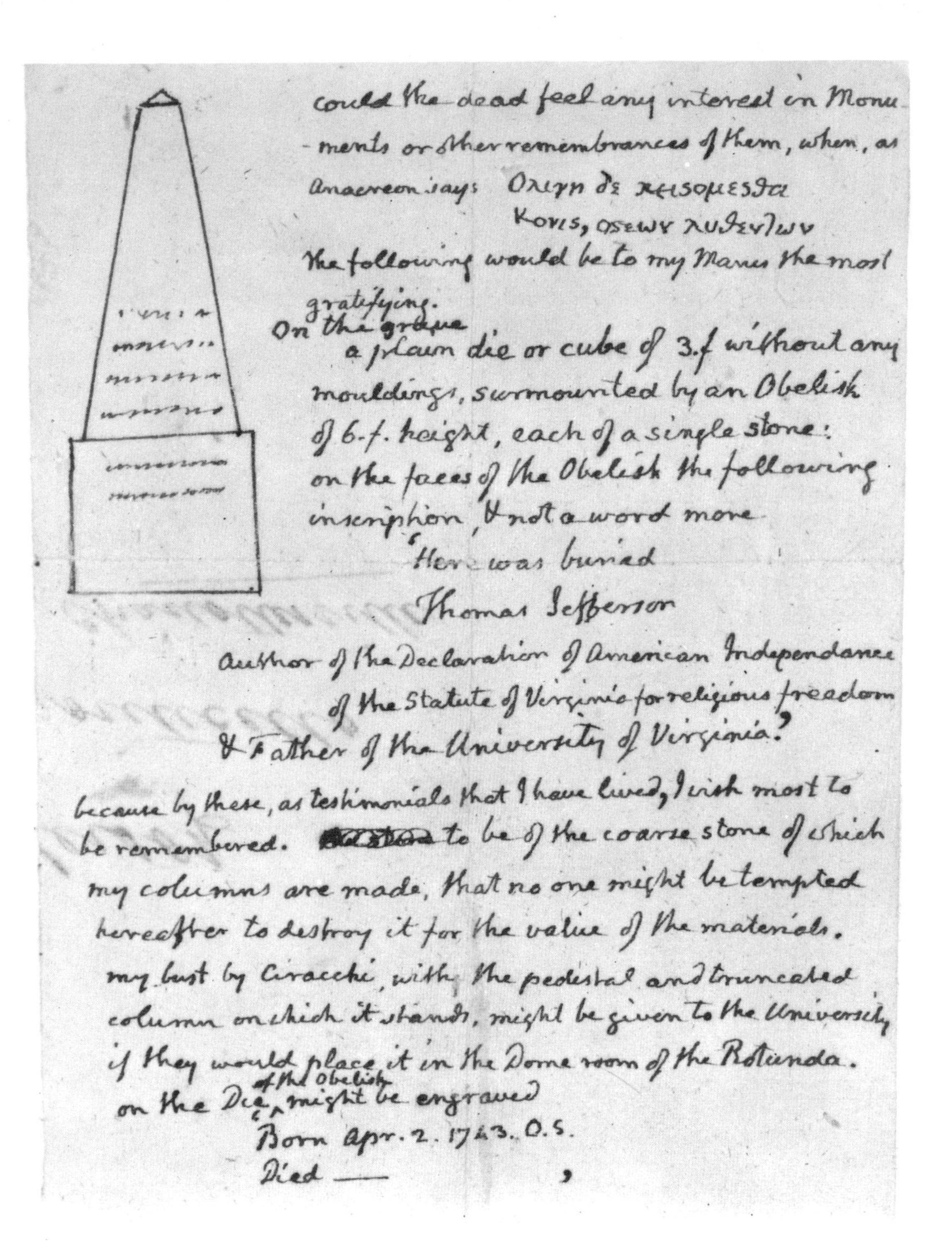

could the dead feel any interest in Monuments or other remembrances of them, when, as Anacreon says Ὀλίγη δὲ κεισόμεσθα κόνις, ὀστέων λυθέντων
the following would be to my Manes the most gratifying.
On the grave
a plain die or cube of 3.f without any mouldings, surmounted by an Obelisk of 6.f. height, each of a single stone:
on the faces of the Obelisk the following inscription, & not a word more

'Here was buried
Thomas Jefferson
Author of the Declaration of American Independance
of the Statute of Virginia for religious freedom
& Father of the University of Virginia.'

because by these, as testimonials that I have lived, I wish most to be remembered. [struck out] to be of the coarse stone of which my columns are made, that no one might be tempted hereafter to destroy it for the value of the materials.
my bust by Ciracchi, with the pedestal and truncated column on which it stands, might be given to the University if they would place it in the Dome room of the Rotunda.
on the Die of the Obelisk might be engraved
Born Apr. 2. 1743. O.S.
Died —— ,

In his Account Book in 1826, Jefferson wrote these instructions for the inscription to be cut on his tombstone, and sketched the "plain die or cube . . . surmounted by an obelisk" he wanted on his grave. He did not note that he had been President of the United States, but wished "most to be remembered" for founding the University of Virginia; and for writing the Declaration of Independence and Virginia's Act for Religious Freedom. The last line should read: Died July 4, 1826.

AMERICAN HERITAGE PUBLISHING CO., INC. • BOOK DIVISION: Richard M. Ketchum, *Editor*. JUNIOR LIBRARY: Ferdinand N. Monjo, *Editor*, John Ratti, *Assistant Editor*. Malabar Schleiter • Judy Sheftel • Julia B. Potts • Mary Leverty, *Editorial Assistants. Designed by Frances Giannoni.*

ACKNOWLEDGMENTS The editors are very grateful to Mr. Dumas Malone, author of *Jefferson and His Time*, for his unfailing assistance; and to Miss Alice Sircom of the Press Bureau of Colonial Williamsburg for her tireless efforts to procure pictorial material for us from the vast collections of that organization. In addition, they wish expressly to thank the following individuals and organizations for their cooperation and assistance: Mrs. Mary D. Kenny and Mrs. Leonard L. Tilman of the Thomas Jefferson Memorial Foundation at Monticello; Mr. Randolph W. Church, State Librarian of the Virginia State Library; Mr. A. L. Dementi of the Dementi Studio in Richmond; Mr. David C. Mearns, Chief of the Manuscripts Division, and Miss Virginia Daiker, Reference Librarian, of the Library of Congress; Miss Gertrude D. Hess, Assistant Librarian of the American Philosophical Society; Mr. Robert E. Stocking of the Alderman Library; Mrs. Edwin Betts of Charlottesville, Virginia; and Mr. Edward S. Jouett of Louisville, Kentucky.

PICTURE CREDITS

The source of each picture used in this book is listed below, by page. When two or more pictures appear on one page, they are separated by semi-colons. The following abbreviations are used:

AL—Alderman Library, University of Virginia
APS—American Philosophical Society
BN—Bibliotheque Nationale, Paris
CW—Colonial Williamsburg
FPG—Freelance Photographers Guild
INHP—Independence National Historical Park
MHS—Massachusetts Historical Society
NG—National Gallery
NG-GC—National Gallery, from the collection of Edgar William & Bernice Chrysler Garbisch
NYHS—New York Historical Society
NYPL—New York Public Library
NYSHA—New York State Historical Association
PUL—Princeton University Library
TJMF—Thomas Jefferson Memorial Foundation (Monticello)
VSL— Virginia State Library

Cover: "The Declaration of Independence," detail, John Trumbull—Yale University Art Gallery. **Front end sheet:** FPG. **Half title:** *Pictorial Field Book to the Revolution*, Benson J. Lossing. **Title:** Charles W. Peale—INHP. **Contents:** "Tobacco Plantation"—CW. **10** NG-GC. **12** (top) *Biography & History of the Indians of North America*, Samuel G. Drake—CW; (bot.) AL. **13** Dementi Studio. **14** AL. **17** *Essay on the Culture & Commerce of Tobacco*, Wm. Tatham —CW. **18** NG-GC. **20** Louis-Alexandre Berthier —PUL. **21** CW. **22** CW. **23** CW. **24** CW. **25** C. W. Peale—CW. **26** Thos. L. Williams. **27** (top) Wm. H. Crossman—CW; (bot.) VSL. **28** CW. **29** Bettman Archives. **30** (top) CW; (bot.) Va. State Capitol. **31** (top) C. W. Peale—INHP; (bot.) Shelburne Museum. **32** (both) Lossing, *op cit.* **33** CW. **34** Coll. Albert F. Smiley; photo courtesy of Hirschl & Adler Galleries. **36** (left) Cook photo—Valentine Museum; (right) State Dept. of Archives & History, N. Ca. **38** Wm. Birch—NYPL. **40** LC. **41** (top) du Simitière— Hist. Soc. Penna; (bot.) MHS. **42** *Designs of Buildings Erected or Proposed*, B. Henry Latrobe —LC. **44** Encyclopaedia Britannica Films. **46** L. L. Beans. **48** Att. to C. W. Peale—CW. **49** Lewis Miller Sketch Books—courtesy VSL. **50** (top) APS; (bot.) PUL. **51** (both) APS. **53** Frederick C. Yohn—Ind. Hist. Bur. **54** Vincennes Memorial. **55** Anon.—Exec. Mansion, Richmond. **56** (top) Virginia Clark Taylor for the Va. Art Commission—VSL; (bot.) courtesy of Edw. S. Jouett. **57** Wm. Ranney—Coll. Dr. J. Lewi Donhauser. **58** *Travels Through the Interior Parts of North America*, Thos. Anburey—NYPL. **60** Thos. L. Williams. **61** MHS. **62** (top) CW; (bot. left) MHS; (bot. right) INHP. **63** NYHS. **64** (both) NYHS. **65** *A Journal of the Operations*, Simcoe—NYPL. **66** "Siege of Yorktown," Louis Van Blarenbergh—Musée de Versailles; courtesy CW. **68** (both) TJMF. **69** *Monticello, Home of Thos. Jefferson*, Randle B. Truett. **70** Coll. Mrs. Charles F. Harrison. **72** Caleb Boyle —Lafayette College, Allan P. Kirby Coll. **74** Wm. L. Clement's Library. **75** LC. **76** Musée de Versailles—Giraudon. **78** Joseph Duplessis— NYHS. **79** (top left) NYSHA; (top right) Fogg Art Museum; (bot.) BN. **80** (top right) Richard Cosway—Henry E. Huntington Library; (top left) Att. to Joseph Boze—American Embassy, Paris, Hugh Campbell Wallace Coll.; (center) BN; (bot. both) Musée de Versailles. **82** Photo Bulloz. **83** *Les Principaux Événemens de la Revolution de Paris*, Ducray du Minil—PUL. **84** BN. **87** The Thomas Jefferson Memorial, Washington. **88** (top to bot.) NYHS; AL; LC. **89** (top to bot.) Thos. L. Williams; Dementi Studio; The Louvre. **90** (top) NYHS; (bot.) TJMF. **91** (all) TJMF. **92** TJMF. **93** (top) NYPL, Arents Coll.; (bot.) The Peale Museum. **94** (all) APS. **95** (top) Harper's Weekly, 1869; (bot. left) Ellen Sharples—National Portrait Gallery, London; (bot. right) TJMF. **96** (top left) The Peabody Museum, by permission of Princeton University Press; (grape & apricot) *Flora & Pompona*, C. McIntosh—NYPL, Arents Coll.;

(olive) New York Botanical Garden; (rice) *The Natural History of Carolina, Florida and the Bahama Islands,* Mark Catesby—NYPL. **97** (top) TJMF; (bot.) MHS. **98** (top left) John H. I. Browere—NYSHA; (bot.) LC. **99** John H. Froehlich—Penna. State Museum. **100** (top to bot.) CW; *A New Book of Nonsense,* W. E. Cresson—LC; *A Portraiture of Domestic Slavery,* Jesse Torrey, Jr.—NYPL. **101** (top left) *Logan the Mingo,* Franklin B. Sawvel—NYPL; APS. **102** Daniel P. Huntington—Brooklyn Museum. **104** LC. **105** AL. **106** BN. **108** Atwater Kent Museum. **109** Ezra Ames—Albany Institute of History & Art. **111** John Trumbull—City Art Commission of New York. **112** NYHS. **113** Chase Manhattan Bank Museum of Moneys of the World. **114** Kennedy—Hist. Soc. of Penna. **115** Wm. Birch—NYPL. **116 & 117**—NYPL. **118** G. Beck—LC. **120** MHS, Coolidge Coll. **121** NYPL, Stokes Coll. **122** Frederick Kemmelmeyer—NG-GC. **124** (top) American Antiquarian Society; (bot.) NYHS. **125** (top) TJMF; (bot.) Dementi Studio. **126** Olds Coll. **128** B. H. Latrobe—Md. Hist. Soc. **130** Mariners' Museum. **132** Att. to Washington Allston—Gibbes Coll. **133** (top) Chase Manhattan Bank; (bot.) Henry E. Huntington Library. **134** Thulstrup—La. Hist. Soc. **135** NG, Samuel H. Kress Coll. **138** Charles Russell—Hist. Soc. of Mont. **139** (top) C. W. Peale—Miss. Hist. Soc.; (bot.) C. W. Peale—INHP. **140** (top) James Audubon—NYPL, Arents Coll.; (bot.) APS. **141** APS. **142** Coll. Mrs. T. Jefferson Coolidge. **145** W. Goodacre—Betts Coll. **146** (top) Catesby, *op. cit.*—NYPL; (bot.) Boze—MHS. **147** (top) Stuart—CW; (bot.) Latrobe—VSL. **149** LC. **Index:** NYPL. **Back end sheet:** FPG. **Back cover:** C. W. Peale—Hist. Soc. of Penna.

BIBLIOGRAPHY

Adams, James Truslow. *The Living Jefferson.* New York: Charles Scribner's Sons, 1936.

Adams, James Truslow. *March of Democracy.* New York: Charles Scribner's Sons, 1932.

Adams, James Truslow. (ed.). *Album of American History.* New York: Charles Scribner's Sons, 1944.

Andrews, Charles M. *The Colonial Period of American History.* New Haven: Yale University Press, 1938.

Beloff, Max. *Thomas Jefferson and American Democracy.* London: Hodder & Stoughton, 1948.

Bodley, Temple. *George Rogers Clark.* Boston: Houghton Mifflin Co., 1926.

Bowers, Claude. *Jefferson and Hamilton.* Boston: Houghton Mifflin Co., 1929.

Bowers. *Jefferson in Power.* Boston: Houghton Mifflin Co., 1936.

Bowers. *The Young Jefferson.* Boston: Houghton Mifflin Co., 1945.

Chinard, Gilbert. *Thomas Jefferson.* Ann Arbor: University of Michigan, 1957.

Davidson, Marshall. *Life in America.* Boston: Houghton Mifflin Co., 1951.

Dos Passos, John. *The Head and Heart of Thomas Jefferson.* Garden City, Doubleday, 1954.

Faulkner, Harold. *American Political and Social History.* New York: Appleton, 1957.

Foster, Genevieve. *George Washington's World.* New York: Charles Scribner's Sons, 1941.

Frary, Ilina Thayer. *Thomas Jefferson, Architect and Builder.* Richmond: Garrett & Massie, Inc., 1950.

Hirst, F. W. *Life and Letters of Thomas Jefferson.* New York: Macmillan, 1926.

Jefferson, Thomas. *Farm Book,* ed. Edwin M. Betts. Philadelphia: American Philosophical Society, 1953.

Jefferson, Thomas. *Garden Book,* ed. Edwin M. Betts. Philadelphia: American Philosophical Society, 1944.

Jefferson. *Jefferson Himself,* ed. Bernard Mayo. Boston: Houghton Mifflin Co., 1942.

Jefferson. *Jefferson Profile: As revealed in his letters,* ed. Saul Padover. New York: John Day, 1956.

Johnson, Allen. *Jefferson and His Colleagues.* New Haven: Yale University Press, 1921.

Kimball, Marie. *Jefferson: The Road to Glory.* New York: Coward-McCann, 1943.

Lisitzky, Gene. *Thomas Jefferson.* New York: Viking Press, 1933.

Malone, Dumas. *Jefferson and the Rights of Man.* Boston: Little, Brown & Co., 1951.

Malone, Dumas. *Jefferson the Virginian.* Boston: Little, Brown & Co., 1948.

Mayo, Bernard. "A Peppercorn for Mr. Jefferson," *Virginia Quarterly* (April, 1943).

National Cyclopaedia of American Biography. New York: James White & Co., 1893.

Padover, Saul. *Jefferson: A Great American's Life and Ideas.* New York: New American Library, 1952.

Parton, James. *Life of Thomas Jefferson.* Boston: Houghton Mifflin Co., 1884.

Problems in American Civilization. (Readings selected by the Dept. of American Studies, Amherst). Boston: D. C. Heath & Co., 1950.

Randolph, Sarah N. *The Domestic Life of Thomas Jefferson.* New York: Frederick Ungar, 1958.

Schachner, Nathan. *The Founding Fathers.* New York: Putnam, 1954.

Schachner. *Thomas Jefferson.* New York: Thomas Yoseloff, 1951.

Thwaites, Reuben G. *How George Rogers Clark Won the Northwest.* Chicago: A. C. McClurg & Co., 1903.

Woodward, William E. *A New American History.* New York: Farrar & Rinehart, 1936.

FOR FURTHER READING

Young readers seeking further information on Thomas Jefferson and his world will find the following books to be both helpful and entertaining:

Acheson, Patricia. *America's Colonial Heritage.* New York: Dodd, Mead & Co., 1957.

Barksdale, Lena. *That Country Called Virginia.* New York: Knopf, 1947.

Bliven, Bruce, Jr. *American Revolution.* New York: Random House, Landmark, 1958.

Briggs, Berta N. *To The Shores of Tripoli.* Philadelphia: Winston, 1955.

Campbell, Charles. *Memoirs of a Monticello Slave.* Charlottesville, Virginia: University of Virginia Press, 1951.

Cook, Fred. *Golden Book of the American Revolution.* New York: Golden Press, 1959.

Fisher, Dorothy Canfield. *Our Independence and the Constitution.* New York: Random House, Landmark, 1950.

Jefferson, Thomas. *The Life and Selected Writings of Jefferson,* ed. Adrienne Koch and William Peden. New York: Random House, The Modern Library, 1944.

Lisitzky, Gene. *Thomas Jefferson.* New York: Viking, 1933.

McGee, Dorothy Horton. *Famous Signers of the Declaration.* New York: Dodd, Mead & Co., 1955.

Miers, Earl S. *Story of Thomas Jefferson.* New York: Grossett & Dunlap, 1955.

Montross, Lynn. *Washington and the Revolution.* Boston: Houghton, Mifflin & Co., 1959.

Neuberger, Richard L. *Lewis and Clark Expedition.* New York: Random House, Landmark, 1951.

Norton, Sybil, and Cournos, John. *John Adams: Independence Forever.* New York: Henry Holt & Co., Inc., 1954.

Rogers, Frances, and Beard, Alice. *Birthday of a Nation: July 4, 1776.* Boston: Lippincott, 1945.

Schachner, Nathan. *Alexander Hamilton: Nation Builder.* New York: McGraw-Hill, 1952.

Sheean, Vincent. *Thomas Jefferson: Father of Democracy.* New York: Random House, Landmark, 1953.

Tallant, Robert. *Louisiana Purchase.* New York: Random House, Landmark, 1952.

INDEX

Bold face *indicates pages on which illustrations appear.*